People are Talking:

Nancy Seiling has a big heart, an equally big smile, and her sense of humour shines through every story in *Amazed! (and Sometimes Dazed)*. Her love of life, family, friends, and God makes you want to spend more time with her. And you can do just that as you read through her stories. Each one will fill you with peace, joy, and a sense of wonder at just how good God really is.

Connie Gibson
Author of the *Nana Murray Has a Farm* Series

Nancy Seiling has done it again. Just as in her first book, *When is Tomorrow? Amazed! (and Sometimes Dazed)* draws us right into the nitty-gritty of her daily life. Readers share the tears and laughter of life along with her. Not even Chronic Fatigue Syndrome could stop her.

One is thankful, along with Nancy, that she found such a perfect partner in David, who not only enhanced her talents but perfectly rounded out the ministry with his own strengths. A fascinating and entirely satisfying read.

Ruth Smith Meyer
Author and Kindred Spirit

How I enjoyed this book! Seiling is a born storyteller and delivers an abundance of tales, all written with a healthy dose of laughter and a deep gratitude for God's presence in her remarkable life. Early in the book, I thought I had found my favourite story. Before long I was thinking, *no, this one is now my favourite.* I'm sure you too will have many favourites as you read and savour this collection of marvelous stories.

Barbara Heagy
Writer/Author, 10 – A Story of Love, Life, and Loss;
Co-Author, Good Grief People

We all have ups and downs in our lives. How we handle them makes the difference. *Amazed! (and Sometimes Dazed)* will empower you to press on. Nancy's writings speak to the heart. You may laugh and you may cry, but you will enjoy this book.

Bob & Dory Hardley
Founders of deCycles

To know the Seilings is to love them; and to meet them is to feel their heart for those in need as you will soon see in *Amazed! (and Sometimes Dazed)*. This delightfully told and eminently readable collection of stories is filled with a wisdom, depth, and humour that will leave your sides splitting and your heart singing. I challenge you: Open it, and just try to put it down!

Dan
Humanitarian Aid Worker

I just romped through Nancy's new book. What a ride! Nancy has a way of making every event come alive. No boredom here. She also has a unique way to attach every experience of life to her personal walk with Jesus. You are sure to thoroughly enjoy *Amazed! (and Sometimes Dazed)*.

Keith Parks
Pastor and Friend

If this book were edible, I would definitely call it *comfort food*! It's what we all need from time to time to satisfy and bring fulfillment to our minds and spirits. But, before digging into the chapters, you must first taste the appetizer—the Foreword. It will prepare you well for the nourishment to follow. Ahhhh yes, good old-fashioned comfort and inspiration, delightful to devour.

George W Grosshans
Watchman, International Educator, Pastor, Friend

Nancy, a small-town girl, has had a big-world impact in her exciting life. Now she continues with her wonderful writing. This book is a delight and encouragement and I highly recommend it.

Paul Shrier, PhD.
Professor of Practical Theology at Azusa Pacific University

To Felica
It is my honour to give you my book. May God bless you as you read of God's faithfulness
Love
Nancy ♥

AMAZED! (AND SOMETIMES DAZED)

How God Used a Small-Town Girl in Big Ways

AMAZED! (AND SOMETIMES DAZED)

How God Used a Small-Town Girl in Big Ways

Nancy Seiling

Amazed! (and Sometimes Dazed); How God Used a Small-Town Girl in Big Ways.

© 2021 Nancy Seiling

All rights reserved. No part of this publication may be reproduced, stored in a retrieval system, or transmitted in any form or by any means—electronic, mechanical, photocopying, recording, or otherwise—without written permission from the copyright holder, except for brief quotations in printed reviews.

Scripture taken from the New King James Version®. Copyright © 1982 by Thomas Nelson. Used by permission. All rights reserved.

First Edition.
ISBN: 978-1-988155-27-2

Angel Hope Publishing
angelhopepublishing@glynisbelec.com

Cover Design by Amanda Belec
@thirteen13designz

Printed in Canada
Innovative Print: innovativeprint.ca

Cover Images: Marco Iwerten
Back cover photo: Queintin Tang

To my wonderful husband, David, who has been my best friend and lover for almost half a century. You were my pillar of strength when I could barely take care of myself. Together we have served God to the best of our abilities, and I've thoroughly enjoyed the journey.

To our sons, Nathan and Matthew, who were a huge part in our ministry. You never complained about the long hours of travel or the countless programs over the years. We are proud of the young men, husbands, and fathers that you have become.

Contents

Acknowledgements i
Foreword iii
Introduction vii
In the Beginning 1
First Memories 3
First Home 5
Hide and Seek 7
New House 9
On the Street Where We lived 11
Life in the Age of "Leave it to Beaver" 13
My Own Room 15
Pretty Flower Girl 17
Not so Good School Days 19
Wonderful Summers 21
Sweet Duets 23
The Dubrick Family 25
New Style of Music 27
Four-Year-Old Jane 29
Family Ties 31
Laughing Family 33
Yukon or Bust 35
Not a Good Year 38
The Funeral 40
More Trials Ahead 42
Funny Dubrick Sisters' Stories 44
High School Days 46
Believing Lies 48
A Ventriloquist is Born 50
First Job 52
Being Miss Nancy 54
Home is Where the Heart Is 56
Wedding in the Family 58
New Opportunity 60
Enter David Seiling 62

Second Date	64
The Joyful Sound	65
Romantic Engagement	67
Another Engagement	69
Wedding Preparations	71
August 4th, 1973 – The Big Day	73
Honeymoon	76
Back to Reality	79
Minister of Youth	81
Funny deCycles' Stories	83
And Then There Were Three	86
Life Can Be A Challenge	88
Our Family Grows	90
Matthew	92
Performing as the Seiling Family	94
100 Huntley Street	95
Thrill of a Lifetime	97
Seiling Family Ministries	100
Dream Home	102
Too Loud Nancy	104
In the Presence of a Star	107
Gotta Love My Husband	109
Love Being a Hostess	111
"And the Rest of You are Angels"	112
Dark Clouds Rising	114
Big Adjustments	116
My Quiet Years	118
Just a Closer Walk With Thee	120
Compelling Vision	122
Laugh or Cry	124
St. Kitts	126
Seoul, South Korea	128
My Favourite Job	130
An Exciting Opportunity	132
A Journey to Africa	134
On the Road	136

Humorous Theatre Antics	138
Girls' Getaway	140
Meaningful Tour for Matthew	142
Matthew and Sarah	144
Dump Story	146
Final Tour	148
A New Ministry Opportunity	149
Joyful Anticipation	151
Hong Kong, Here We Come!	152
Time Flies	154
I Need Clean Clothes!	156
Samara and Taylor	158
Tanya's Surprise Birthday Party	161
Imitation	163
Return to Hong Kong	164
Cute Charity Stories	166
Difficult News from Home	168
Philippines Break or What?	170
Free Time	172
All Things Come to an End	174
Never Hurts to Laugh	176
Jane's Release to Heaven	178
Honduras Opportunity	180
deCycles Staff	182
Third Generation Ventriloquist	184
Difficult Decisions	186
Mom's Release to her Heavenly Home	188
Final Goodbye	189
Funny David	191
I'm Faster Than You Are!	192
Beautiful Dream of my Mama	194
Emotional Decisions	196
An Adorable Child	198
Coincidences Galore	200
Summer Cottage	202
No One's Perfect	204

Hero!	206
Confession is Good for the Soul	208
Backpack vs. Boulders	210
Chance Meeting	212
Civic Duty	214
Being Honest	216
How Did Tomorrow Become Yesterday?	218
Covid-19	220
What is Ahead?	222
About the Author	224

Acknowledgements

It takes a village to raise a child.
African Proverb

We need each other all through life, and that is a good thing. Each one of us brings something different to relationships and each talent is needed. I could not have written this book without help.

My son Nathan has proved invaluable with his computer skills. Whenever I hit a snag, I call him for help, and he answers saying, "I.T. for Old People!" He always solves my problems so I can continue to write. What would I have done without you?

David is my proofreader. He catches missed words, commas out of place, and often offers helpful suggestions. Thank you honey.

My family is my treasure. Our family gatherings are filled with much laughter, and good food. Thank you for your love and support.

Many thanks to my editor Glynis Belec. Once again, you've made me look better than I am. I thank you for your patience and kind explanations when you wielded your red pen on my manuscript.

Above all, I thank my loving Heavenly Father who blessed me with an amazing life. Serving You has given me adventures I could never have dreamed possible.

Foreword

I heard a loud, bubbly "Hello! We're here!" followed by a cheerful laughter from upstairs. *Who could that be?* I thought to my eight-year-old self. There was such excitement in her greeting. I had never heard such meaningful and heartfelt laughter before. This laughter sounded genuinely happy, but not just happy—joyful; filled with passion and a spirit that was brighter than most.

Being so young at the time, I guess I hadn't heard much laughter. But there was something different and unique about what I was hearing from this person. It was the type of sound that just drew me to the source, making me want more; a kind of positivity and light that filled me to the brim with pleasure, hard to find these days. An encouraging kind of laughter reminding me that life was great and that I had so much to be thankful for.

If you heard this laughter, it would put a smile on your face, too, and just being in the presence of this person would turn your bad day around filling you with happiness and good vibes. You would leave assured about how there are amazing things awaiting you in this world, and you would leave hopeful of something bigger and more for yourself; like you matter; like you are loved and worthy. You would leave dazed, wondering about genuine kindness and sincere character. Not many people leave that impression.

I couldn't put my finger on what it was then or what it all meant, but now, at 15 years of age, I believe it was the Holy Spirit inside my Nana. I believe she has always borne spiritual fruit. No person is perfect. No one demonstrates the Fruits of the Spirit[1] all the time. But I believe my Nana really does try and she mostly succeeds. My Nana is unlike any other. If you've met my Nana Nancy and have had the privilege of spending some time with her, then you know what I mean.

Maybe you are wondering why I was only eight years old when I met my Nana for the first time. I met her at my foster parents' home. I came from a broken family and was put into the foster care

---

[1] "But the fruit of the Spirit is love, joy, peace, longsuffering, kindness, goodness, faithfulness, gentleness, self-control. Against such there is no law." Galatians 5:22-23 NKJV

system. I had been an only child with biological parents who were always fighting, yelling, and swearing. My parents were addicted to many illegal street drugs and drank alcohol. They committed other crimes, like thievery and were in and out of jail. My birth mother was a prostitute at one time. We didn't have much money and eventually lost our apartment and ended up homeless. My mom and I were in and out of different homeless shelters for months, until I ended up being left at my biological grandmother's home. She arranged for me to go into foster care, knowing it would be best. That's when I met the Seiling family.

Matt (Nancy's youngest son) and his wife, Sarah, took me in with open arms even with two children of their own—Launa who was six at the time and Trenton was three. I was in foster care under their roof for two years. When I was 10 years old, the paperwork was done, and adoption became an option. The Seilings were asked if they would like to adopt me. We already felt like family and everyone agreed they wanted me to be a part of their family officially. It was so amazing to officially become part of a real, loving family. Getting my last name changed to "Seiling" was the final step. Now, almost six years later, I am happy to be called a member of the Seiling family. My life is forever changed in so many ways because of them.

As I read in *Amazed! (and Sometimes Dazed)* about the family my Nana grew up in, then the family my Daddy grew up in, it made me realize what a privilege it was to grow up in a solid, stable, Christian home; something I yearned for often.

Seeing how they were raised and the impact that a secure household and environment had on their lives at a young age spoke volumes about how good parenting and family life can shape your future. It made me grateful to be out of that terrible childhood situation and how appreciative I was to be adopted into the Seiling family. My new parents allowed me to enjoy even a portion of my childhood, and the love of the Seiling family transformed me from a place of sadness to a lifetime of joy, surrounded by people who cared about me; who wanted the best for me; who hoped I would chase after God and draw near to Him forever. Nana Nancy Seiling was and still is one of my biggest cheerleaders.

Nana taught me that life is wonderful. It is full of goodness; full of ups and downs; positivity and greatness. Life really is amazing. We have to do what we can to make the most of it and live it to the fullest. There are going to be hardships, things to overcome. It can get pretty messy and ugly at times. Sometimes it might seem there is no way out of the darkness.

But there is! In Nana Nancy's book *Amazed! (and Sometimes Dazed),* she tells unique and impactful stories about her journey through life. You *will* be amazed meeting Nancy beginning at her remarkable birth all the way up to her life now in 2021. You will continue to be amazed as you read about her different experiences.

Nancy demonstrates that there is a way out of the hard times. She reveals how life is like a roller coaster. So many ups and downs. She taught me that no one and no life is perfect, but when you have a positive attitude and an optimistic outlook, when you love Jesus and follow His plan and let Him use you, and when you try your best to help others and serve those in need, just like my Nana does, it makes everything a whole lot easier!

Some of her stories will make you laugh, make you thankful, and fill you with joy. Other stories will make you cry as you read about aspects of her life and the memories she shares. You will see where God took her after these years and what her special purpose and gifts are. Her stories are and will be forever affecting.

In every situation, Nana Nancy brings God into the picture and connects either a Bible lesson or a life lesson to tuck away.

Just like Nancy has a purpose, so do I. You have a purpose too. Everyone does. I pray as you read about these divine moments in Nancy's life, you would know God can use *you* in big ways as well.

Be blessed as you dive into Nancy Seiling's life-changing stories and testimony, and know that God too, can take you somewhere grand.

Breana ♥

Breana Seiling, 15 years
Grateful High School Student, Happy Granddaughter

Introduction

My first book, *When Is Tomorrow? A Devotional for Caregivers*, was a labour of love written in memory of my mother, Flo Kufske. Ever since that book was published, I knew there had to be at least one more deep inside me. Turns out, there was!

If anyone would have told me, little Nancy Dubrick, about the adventures that awaited, I never would have believed them. However, God must have been smiling because He, alone, knew the future and He had an amazing plan for me and my family.

Let me be clear. I did nothing to deserve my life, but oh how thankful I was to God for blessing me with so many adventures.

There have been highs and lows; struggles and laughter; pain and joy. Through it all, a loving Heavenly Father guided me. Far from perfect, I have made some bad decisions, and taken some wrong turns along the way. But in the midst of it all, God was faithful. He forgave me for my failures and gently led me back onto the right path. God gave me the desires of my heart through a loving, strong, but gentle husband, two wonderful sons, two beautiful daughters-in-law, and five exceptional grandchildren. And adventures! Let me tell you about some of them.

Get yourself a nice cup of your favourite warm beverage, put your feet up, and let's travel down memory lane together. You'll get a front row seat and see where it all began. Join me on my journey—a wild ride that took me to many countries of the world, in God's service.

In the Beginning

> *Then the word of the LORD came to me, saying: "Before I formed you in the womb I knew you; Before you were born I sanctified you; ..."*
> **Jeremiah 1:4-5a**

I've always wondered why I haven't mastered the art of gliding into a room like a lady. Why can't I just sit down, fold my hands demurely in my lap, and smile sweetly? I suppose I could do that if I really forced myself. Instead, my natural tendency is to walk into a room with a not-so-subtle, "ta da!" I feel the need to connect and immediately begin talking with someone, otherwise I feel a bit foolish. It's even better if I can make people laugh. It is especially nice when I arrive and my friends say, "Oh good, Nancy's here. Now we can laugh!"

Wait a minute ... now that I think about it, perhaps they're laughing at me, not with me! Hmmm. That changes things a tad, doesn't it? Might not be a compliment after all. Oh well, I will choose to continue to look at it as a compliment, if you don't mind, and carry on.

Perhaps my need for attention stems from my birth. I made quite a scene when I entered the world, apparently, and quickly gained a lot of attention from the nurses and doctors. I've often wondered if that was just a small sample of who I would become.

When Mom went into labour near her due date, Daddy (my forever nickname for my father) took her to the hospital. Back in 1950, fathers weren't allowed in the birthing room with their wives, so Mom was by herself. Things were going along nicely until, suddenly, she began hemorrhaging. What happened next sent the staff scurrying. Placenta Previa, which meant the placenta was coming first. This necessitated an emergency C-section to save both of us. I never did find out what Daddy went through during all the commotion, but suffice to say, it was touch and go for a while, according to what I was told.

Mom often told me I was gorgeous, even at birth. No pictures of me as a newborn to prove it, though. I felt put out about that. I mean, here I am gorgeous for once in my life, but not one picture to prove it. Guess you'll just have to take my mother's word for it.

After an appropriate time in the hospital, Daddy took Mother and baby Nancy home. And just like that, three-year-old Janet had a new sister.

Doesn't it fill you with peace knowing that God knew us even before we were formed in our mother's womb? He alone knew the date of our birth and He also knows the date of our death. He chose when we would be born and who our parents would be. He also has a great plan for our lives.

*Me at nine months of age.
Get a load of that crop of hair!*

First Memories

For God so loved the world that He gave His only begotten Son, that whoever believes in Him should not perish but have everlasting life. **John 3:16**

At five years of age, when visiting my grandparent's farm, Grandma taught me about heaven and sin.
"My little Nancy. God is your best Friend. And He lives in a special place called Heaven."

My eyes opened wide. "Where is it?" I wondered.

Grandma went on to tell me about a perfect heaven, but she also told me about sin and how sad it made God when we did bad things. She told me that God did not allow sin in heaven.

I knew my track record, even at the tender age of five. I stuck out my bottom lip and worried about my options. In my young mind, I wasn't heading to Heaven because I had done a lot of bad things.

"Grandma, what do I have to do to go to Heaven someday?"

"Nancy, Jesus did the hard part when He died on the cross. He took our sins onto Himself and all we have to do is admit that we have sinned and accept His gift of salvation."

That sounded easy enough.

"Would you like to pray and accept God's free gift?" Grandma asked. I readily agreed. We knelt and I prayed a simple child's prayer and even though I didn't totally understand, I knew something important had happened.

"Your name is now in the Lamb's Book of Life," Grandma told me, and I was filled with peace. Grandma had to chuckle though when I proudly declared to my family, "Grandma saved me!"

Grandma was then quick to add, "No Nancy, Grandma didn't save you. Jesus did."

Although this happened decades ago, it is still fresh in my mind and I shall never forget that moment. It turned out to be the first big decision that would last a lifetime.

Do you have a story that you recall that changed your life? This picture is imprinted into my mind, and I am forever thankful for a praying Grandmother. Even a child can make a decision to follow Jesus. We are never too old or too young to be prepared for Heaven.

1954

<u>Front Row</u> *Left to Right: Nancy Dubrick, Wayne Leis, Bob Litwiller, Janet Dubrick, Gloria Litwiller.*
<u>2nd Row</u>: *Ron Litwiller.*
<u>3rd Row</u> *Left to Right: Grandma Emma Litwiller, Grandpa Herb Litwiller, Florence (Mom) Dubrick, Wilfred (Dad) Dubrick, Doris Leis, Elmer Leis.*
<u>4th Row</u> *Left to Right: Joyce Kranz, Len Litwiller, Barb Litwiller, Jim Litwiller (baby), Vietta Litwiller, Stan Litwiller, Rita Litwiller, Art Litwiller.*

First Home

Through wisdom a house is built, And by understanding it is established. **Proverbs 24:3**

I clearly remember everything about the first little apartment where I lived with my family. In my 5-year-old mind's eye I can still picture the long set of stairs straight up to our living space. My great grandparents on Daddy's side had renovated their beautiful two-story home into three apartments for family members. Even now, I sometimes dream I am walking up those high stairs and wandering through that little apartment. I remember the attic where I'd often go and look through all the delightful things stored up there. One of the treasures turned out to be an old, hand-cranked phonograph with a record about Noah and the big ark. I loved to be deliciously scared when the reader on the record would say, "And God shut the big door." BANG! The loud thud never failed to make me jump, but I'd still go back time and again to crank up the sound.

Although *I* recall my first home vividly, my husband David, on the other hand, doesn't. He cannot remember what the house looked like that he lived in from age five until age 10.

"I figure we must have had a kitchen, because we ate!" he would say. He also recalls the time his parents locked themselves out. "I had to squeeze through the milk box and drop into the kitchen to unlock the door, so, yes, there must have been a kitchen."

David's parents moved often. When he came into this world, David's family lived in Waterloo. His brother Ronald, 15 months, at the time, would say, "I live at two-sicky-four Hazel Street." Everyone would chuckle at the cuteness. When David turned five, they moved to Kitchener. By his tenth birthday, they moved to Elmira, and at age 15 they moved to the farm. David always says, "My parents moved every five years, but I'd eventually find them. I'd go knocking on doors and ask, 'Did you see my mommy and daddy?'" The people would say, "What are their names little boy?" and David would answer, "Mommy and Daddy!" Of course, that never happened, but it makes a funny story to tell and David is rewarded with laughter. To finish the story, David likes to add, "So when I was 20, I moved, but they never came looking for me!"

Do you remember your childhood? What event do you first recall? Take a minute and go down memory lane. You may be surprised at what surfaces.

David and his father, with a big catch.

Hide and Seek

"What do you think? If a man has a hundred sheep, and one of them goes astray, does he not leave the ninety-nine and go to the mountains to seek the one that is straying? And if he should find it, assuredly, I say to you, he rejoices more over that sheep than over the ninety-nine that did not go astray. **Matthew 18:12-13**

When you are three years old, playing outside, and you get the urge to go to the bathroom, you need to go. Right away! I didn't remember that happening to me, but I think it must have, because I have been reminded of that day often over the years. Apparently, because I didn't want to climb the long staircase to our apartment, I ended up wetting my pants. This embarrassed me and I didn't want Mom to know, so I climbed into the basement window well at the side of the house to hide. Soon, I fell asleep. Mom came to look for me. "Nancy, time to come inside. Where are you?"

When I didn't answer, she became concerned. She checked with my friends and walked the whole neighborhood, but no Nancy. Mom called Daddy at work. He rushed home to help with the search. Frantic now, they called the police. Neighbours rallied to help. Mom stayed on the front porch watching and praying. Suddenly, Mom heard what sounded like a kitten meowing. She hurried around the corner of the house and spotted me in the window well, crying. Mom gave thanks to God and hoisted me out. The lost had been found. Everyone rejoiced when they heard the news.

I don't think anyone cared that I had wet my pants. I do vaguely recall this incident, but of course, did not realize the panic that I caused my parents.

Just so you know, I never did that again (wet my pants or fall asleep in a window well).

Not until I was a mother myself, did I totally understand the anxiety that Mom and Daddy must have felt at the time. I never did find out how long I was missing. Although it was long enough to organize a search party.

This reminds me of the story of the lost lamb. The Good Shepherd searched and searched until He found this wandering little one, and lovingly carried it home. We can be assured that no matter what we've done, or how far we've strayed, our Good Shepherd is willing to search for us and take us back. We may have hit rock bottom, but He is always there saying, "Welcome back to the fold."

Grandma Dubrick with her four daughters.
Left to Right: Marie, Alice, Grandma, Evelyn, Gladys.

Daddy's family.
Front Row Left to Right: Evelyn, Alice, Marie, Gladys.
Back row L-R Grandpa, Garfield, Leonard, Milton, Howard, Wilfred (my daddy).

New House

"Honor your father and mother," which is the first commandment with promise: **Ephesians 6:2**

Five-years-olds don't always understand what is going on around them. I can't ever recall my parents telling me we were moving, nor did I notice packed boxes surrounding us. I must have been in my own little world. Our apartment had a tiny bathroom with a small tub that would have suited any one of the seven dwarfs nicely. The bathroom in our new house seemed huge to me and had shiny black tiles. The tub appeared to be three times the size as the one in the apartment. I marvelled at the wonder of it all. Then I found out that this house belonged to us. Imagine! Not only that, but our school was only nine houses away and Janet and I could easily walk there on our own.

To our delight, we discovered many children our age lived in the neighborhood. We soon made lots of friends and spent many enjoyable hours together. Turned out we had the only house on the street with a paved driveway, so everyone congregated at our place to play skipping, especially Double Dutch, our favourite. Before long, we became quite proficient at it.

My sisters and I were the heroes of the neighbourhood and we didn't do anything but live in a house with a paved driveway. We felt like we were some kind of celebrities with everyone wanting to come to the Dubrick house to play.

Years later I remember being in a car with someone who was trying to sell a pyramid scheme to David and me. He took us on a tour of different neighbourhoods. We passed blocks of smaller homes similar to the ones David and I both grew up in, and then we travelled to the richer section of town.

"You won't have to ever consider living in dinky homes like that if you get involved with our company." The sales pitch referring to the small homes grated on our better judgement.

David and I knew this proposition was not for us. Their motto, *Money is Everything*, certainly did not match our experience.

I remember thinking, *But I grew up in one of those supposedly inferior small homes and had a great childhood.*

I wish now that I would have voiced how I felt. There are many happy people living in small homes, as well as unhappy people in large homes. The reverse can also be true of course, but the fact is, the size of the house isn't important, but the family dynamics are the key. A home should never be measured by what part of town it is in or by the square footage. Our family may not have been wealthy, but we were rich in what was most important. We loved each other, had lots of relatives who truly enjoyed being together and laughed easily. What more could we have needed?

On the Street Where We lived

If it is possible, as much as depends on you, live peaceably with all men. **Romans 12:18**

Only one side of our street had a sidewalk, and luckily for us, it happened to be on our side. This meant we could go back and forth in front of our house with our roller skates as much as we wanted. Of course, back then our skates clipped onto our shoes and we had a key to tighten them. I think we spent more time putting them back on after they fell off than actually skating, but we didn't get discouraged. We'd skate, stop, tighten, and go a bit farther, only to have to tighten the skate over again. Not sure if we were tenacious or just plain dumb to put up with it but put up with it, we did.

I recall the time Daddy first taught me how to ride a bicycle. He'd hang on and run beside me. I would beg him not to let go. However, for me to learn, he had to. I may have fallen a couple of times but oh, the thrill of knowing that I was doing this all on my own!

My bicycle was my prized possession. Mom used to tell us how she longed for a bicycle when she was young, but her parents could not afford one. This made us treasure our bicycles even more.

Our parents rarely said, "I love you," but they proved it each day. Mom stayed at home, and Daddy worked. We weren't unique, though, as many of my friends had this arrangement in their families too. I did have one friend who had no brothers or sisters. Both her parents worked. I remember even at a young age feeling sorry for her for being alone so often.

"Mom, we're home!" were the first words we'd utter the moment we walked through the door after school. Many times we could tell by the delicious smells coming from the kitchen that she had already started supper. We drooled on the days she baked her delicious cinnamon buns. What a treat. To this day, my mind drifts back to that house whenever I smell cinnamon buns. It's funny how cinnamon buns reminds me of the love and security I felt back then.

Not everyone has the same loving memories of home as I experienced. I get that. Our lives were not perfect, but I am thankful for a good foundation.

If you lacked the love and support when you were a child, know that our loving Heavenly Father picks up the pieces, puts you back together again, and makes your life into a thing of beauty. You should not be bound by your past, but with God's help, you can make a better future.

The Dubrick Sisters' Roller Derby. August 1960.

Life in the Age of "Leave it to Beaver"

This hope we have as an anchor of the soul, both sure and steadfast, ... **Hebrews 6:19a**

Many times, I've thanked God I was born in 1950. Our parents were not concerned about allowing us to go places on our own. It was a different time, and everyone kept an eye out for each other. In fact, when I was eight years old and my sister, Janet, was eleven, the two of us would take the bus to attend the Kids' Club on Friday nights at our church, in the heart of our downtown.

At Kid's Club we learned Bible lessons and verses, but Janet and the older girls were also allowed to go into the church kitchen to learn how to bake. Oh, the smells that permeated the rest of the building! They also got to eat the rewards of their hard work, but we younger ones could only imagine how delicious it must have tasted.

I remember wanting desperately to be older so I, too, could be in that kitchen and enjoy the fruits of my labour. We totally loved that club and at 8:30 p.m. we'd leave the church and stand on King Street right across from our beautiful City Hall waiting for the bus to take us home. No one thought anything about it. In the winter, of course, it was already dark even before we left home, but no one was concerned. We loved that our bus stop happened to be right in front of the "The Nut Shack." We'd go in each week armed with our nickels and each buy a small bag of cheese popcorn. Oh my, what a treat that was. Once in a while, Mom would give us extra money to buy some caramel popcorn to bring home to share.

Years later, when I taught six and seven-year-old girls at the Pioneer Club at our church, I made sure they would be able to work in the church kitchen, even though they were young. I remembered that feeling of being left out.

In the winter, the janitors and parent volunteers at our school made sure we had an outdoor skating rink. We all spent many happy hours in the cold. Our feet would be frozen by the time we decided to go home. But no one cared. Having fun was the main thing.

To make things even more exciting, at the end of our long street, there happened to be a dead end that stopped at a hill. Kids dragged their toboggans up and slid down that hill while we squealed and laughed for hours. The walk home always seemed longer than the walk there. Sometimes Mom had hot chocolate waiting to help us thaw out. In summer we played baseball at the school ball diamond. Life couldn't be better.

As adults, we can have the honour of helping others as people have done in our past; like my parents helped us, along with the school janitors and volunteers, and those who looked out for us, when we didn't even know it. *Paying it Forward* is the popular term today. And I like it. Sometimes we do unto others, or perhaps we even try to do things better and differently than what was done for us. And that's a good thing. Not only does the recipient of a good deed benefit, so does the giver. Pay it forward to someone in need today and I am pretty sure you will feel richer for it.

My Own Room

> *Blessed be the God and Father of our Lord Jesus Christ, the Father of mercies and God of all comfort,* **2 Corinthians 1:3**

When Mom and Dad bought the house, the attic was unfinished, so they decided to make two bedrooms up there. One for Janet and one for me. Imagine. I'd get my own room! To this day, I have warm fuzzies whenever I think about having my very own room.

Years later at a wedding shower I attended, instructions for a game included having each of us picture the most important room in the house where we grew up. The idea was for us to share what made it special. I was the last one in the circle to share and the only one to say, "My bedroom."

Janet and I had felt very grown up when were allowed to pick the paint colour for our rooms. I had picked turquoise, thinking it was the most divine color ever. I knew mom would be painting our rooms and I couldn't wait to get home from school that day to see it. To my dismay it wasn't the colour I had wanted. A drab, ordinary green covered my new bedroom. No speck of blue and definitely no turquoise. Mom soon realized this colour was not what I asked for and said she would change it. I didn't want to make extra work for anyone, so I said, "No. It's fine." Deep down inside I was disappointed, but I did not want to hurt my parents by saying so.

I must admit that it didn't hurt me at all to live in a green room, and soon I barely noticed it. Every afternoon when I came home from school, I'd go directly to my room. I would do my homework, relax, listen to music, or read. Then I would change clothes and run outside to play with my friends. I needed that "down time".

Even now, with my bubbly personality, I expend a lot of energy, and need to recoup before going on to the next project.

I always kept my room neat. I took great pride in having all my clothes properly hung up or put away in drawers, my shoes lined up carefully, and my bed perfectly made. Nothing could ever be out of place. I liked it that way. We'd heard lots of stories growing up of how Mom had to share a room with her sister and what chaos that created. Mom was the neat-freak. My Aunt couldn't have cared less. This, apparently, led to many loud arguments that sometimes brought their father into the equation. They hated when he showed up because he was a hard man and often an unreasonable taskmaster. Sadly, even this never permanently resolved their differences.

I still need to have everything neat and tidy or I can't think! *Everything has its place* is my motto, but I married a man whose motto has a different perspective. *If I can't see it, how can I find it?* They say that opposites attract and that is us for sure. Even with such disagreements David and I have a fantastic marriage. Besides, its fun making up afterwards. I've learned to turn a blind eye to some things, and David has learned to put away (hide) most of his mess. It isn't perfect, but it works.

Do you need down time? If you are an "A-type" personality, it is easy to keep going until you drop. However, that can be dangerous. God made our bodies to rest at least one day out of seven. He did this for our benefit, for He knows we can wear ourselves out. When you do rest, don't feel guilty. Look at it as "recharging your batteries" instead. Once you are fully charged, then you can hit the road running once again.

Pretty Flower Girl

Keep me as the apple of Your eye; Hide me under the shadow of Your wings, **Psalm 17:8**

We were just getting settled in our new home when my cousin Shirley on Daddy's side, asked if I would be the flower girl at her wedding. It was all very exciting, because being Shirley's flower girl meant I would be getting a new dress. I vaguely recall being in a bridal store with Shirley and the bridesmaids to pick out the dress. It was gorgeous! All the wedding photos are in black and white, but I do recall my new dress being a pretty pink color. The hem had scallops with many crinolines underneath. A sparkly headband completed my ensemble. I felt like a princess.

Although I have no recollection of the church at all, I must have walked down the aisle without incident. After the ceremony and pictures, the wedding party, including me, went to visit Shirley's grandmother in the hospital. Because of my age, I had to wait outside. But I did get to see her looking down from the second story hospital window. When we returned to the reception, I got to sit at the head table with all the adults. Boy, did I feel special. In front of me was a glass with what I thought was grape juice, so I took a sip. Immediately I knew this was not grape juice. I heard someone gasp. I'd never tasted wine before, but instinctively figured out, "This ain't no grape juice!" No one was angry with me, of course, but I was embarrassed and put my head down on the table until I cooled down.

I'm pretty sure my ego grew when I was asked for the second time to be the flower girl for my Aunt Joyce's wedding a few months later. Once again, I donned my princess gown and crown.

I was still five years old and adorably cute. One glitch, this time. I was close to my Aunt Joyce and had a crush on her fiancée. He was tall dark and handsome and had always been kind to me. In fact, I felt devastated that he chose Aunt Joyce over me! But I got over it. That day went off without a hitch because I'd done this before.

Besides that, there was no alcohol at that wedding, so no mistakes on my part (much to my relief).

Some memories are just too cute not to remember. Being a princess for two weddings thrilled my little girl heart. I have often wondered what happened to my pretty pink flower girl dress.

Can you recall a wonderful memory where you felt special? If nothing comes to mind, remember that you are always special in God's eyes and to add to that delight, you are precious in His sight. We cannot earn this amazing love. It is a gift given to every one of us. A good reason to celebrate.

Pretty Flower Girl.

Not so Good School Days

Then God saw everything that He had made, and indeed it was very good.... **Genesis 1:31a**

Back in the 1950s, teachers were taught to stand by their desk or at the chalkboard to teach. For the general population, this was a great way to learn, but for someone like me who needed a hands-on or a more object-lesson type teaching, that typical teaching method didn't work.

Even to this day, when I listen to a lecture, I learn better if I doodle. There's something about scribbling on a page that helps me concentrate. Sometimes I'd pick up a pencil and begin doodling while the teacher began the lesson. I was then able to concentrate on every word, but she would say, "Nancy, put your pencil down." I would obey, but then my mind would instantly wander. I didn't want it to wander, it just did.

One time, in school, when I was supposed to be listening to the lesson, my mind went to an interesting place. An odd progression took over my thinking and it had nothing to do with the lesson.

Walking is faster than standing;
Roller skates are faster than walking;
a bicycle is faster than roller skates;
a motorcycle is faster than a bicycle;
a car is faster than a motorcycle;
a train is faster than a car;
a plane is faster than a train,
and a rocket is faster than a plane.

After I'd processed this mind-blowing revelation, the teacher finished the lesson, and I hadn't a clue what she had taught. However, I had cemented in my mind, the different modes of transportation, and how fast each one of them moved compared to the other. Now that was important. At least I thought so! I am sure I failed the next test, but even all these decades later, I recall that sequence. Probably no one else in that class or even the teacher herself could say that they remembered that particular lesson that she taught that day either, so I feel rather special.

We all have a defining moment in our lives. For some of us, there may have been more than one, but usually we can look back on one particular incident knowing that it framed our thoughts and actions.

My defining moment happened when the teacher handed out some papers and said, "This test will separate the sheep from the goats." We all understood she meant the ones who pass are sheep, and the ones who fail are goats. I failed that test. It stands out as clearly now as it did over 50 years ago. From that moment on, I had proof of my stupidity, and nothing would change my mind. I would envy all the smart kids and wonder how it must feel to ace every exam while I barely got by. My low self-esteem plummeted even further.

I have never shared this story with anyone, not even my parents. It's not as if they would have been angry with me, but we simply did not discuss our feelings. I do remember telling them that I hated school, but nothing else. Now I wish that I would have been more open and admitted to them how that teacher made me feel. Perhaps they could have helped me at home, or had a discussion with the teacher, but I kept it to myself. It also would have made a huge difference if someone would have suggested I write my feelings down in a journal. Instead, I suffered in silence.

Can you relate? Is there a defining moment in your life that negatively impacted you and one that you will forever remember? Have you been able to get past that, or do those words or actions still reverberate in your mind? The good news is, although none of us can go back and change the past, we can change the way we see ourselves now. Ask God to remove that bad memory or memories and replace them with His love. He looks at us with compassion and caring when we allow Him into our lives.

Wonderful Summers

Therefore do not worry about tomorrow, for tomorrow will worry about its own things. Sufficient for the day is its own trouble.
Matthew 6:34

I always appreciated that I could celebrate my birthday in June (June 12th to be exact—just in case you want to send me a birthday gift.)
A June birthday meant there were only two weeks of school left. Those last weeks were filled with lots of good things, including going to a stadium for the city-wide track-and-field competitions. I may not have been an athlete, but I sure did know how to whoop and holler for those who were competing for our school. We usually had some kind of "end of school" class party where the teacher would give us a small treat and we'd have fun the whole day. It was fantastic, especially when we looked forward to two whole months of freedom! As the song says, "It's the Most Wonderful Time of the Year"—at least it was for me.

My family loved to do things together in the summer. Our large backyard was perfect for extended family picnics. Each family would bring a basket of food and we'd pool it together and stuff ourselves, laughing all the while. Not too many people had BBQs on our street back in the 50s, but we still enjoyed amazing food.

One time, my daddy showed off by doing some tricks he'd learned on a bicycle. We were all on the front lawn watching, when suddenly, the front wheel detached from the bike as Daddy lifted the handlebars. Of course, with the wheel gone, the bike did a nosedive and Daddy landed unceremoniously on the cement. Fortunately, the only thing wounded was his pride, and when he laughed, we all laughed along with him.

Sometimes our family went fishing or camping. For our first camping trip, someone lent us a tent, and we left to try it out right after Daddy came home from work. Trouble began as soon as we arrived at the campground. Darkness enveloped us by the time we found our campsite and the air was thick with mosquitoes. Everyone seemed to be in a bad mood until finally, after some struggles, the adults put up the tent. We felt a little better as we wearily climbed in for the night, still swatting at pesky mosquitoes until we fell asleep.

It wasn't until morning that my parents saw why they had had so much trouble setting up the tent. It was inside out! Oh my, did they laugh. The rest of the camping trip went well.

I especially liked how we could go barefoot in the little campground store. I can still feel the soft sand on the soles of my feet that hundreds of others had dragged in. We'd searched for pop bottles left behind from other campers and cashed them in for two cents each. What to do with all those pennies? It didn't take long for us to figure it out—candy! We were sure we had hit the jackpot! Such fond memories.

I like this quote by Jim and Terry Kraus: "One must write to remember. An unremembered life will come to vapor at the end. Stories need to be told."

One does not have to be an author to write about memorable experiences. Write your stories down. Hang on to them and bring them out from time to time to remind yourself that there is still some good in the world and many reasons to laugh.

Sweet Duets

Let no one despise your youth, but be an example to the believers in word, in conduct, in love, in spirit, in faith, in purity.
1 Timothy 4:12

Music has been an integral part of my life ever since I can remember. When I turned five, a friend of my parents heard me sing. Impressed, this friend, who was also connected to a local radio station, wanted my parents to sign a contract for me to sing on the radio. They refused. Too bad. I could have been a star!

Later our church saw potential in my sister, Janet, and me when we were still young. Janet, who was nine at the time, took accordion lessons. Her natural talent allowed her to excel quickly. By the time she was ten and I was seven, we started singing duets together. Mom carefully chose the songs for us to sing in our Sunday School open sessions. The Pastor heard us one Sunday and invited us to sing in the regular church service. Immediately he discovered that the congregation loved these two little girls on stage singing their hearts out. I can't imagine that we could have been very good, but this gave us the opportunity we needed to gain confidence and poise in front of an audience.

Our church had stairs behind the platform and Janet and I would always slip down them after we sang. As we traversed downward, we'd quietly discuss the mistakes we made. But there came a time when we excitedly whispered, "We didn't make one mistake!" What an accomplishment.

Our grandmother saw something special—a unique talent in her two young granddaughters. She would occasionally take us on the bus to the Kitchener-Waterloo Hospital, as it was called at the time, to sing in the hallways for seniors on the long-term wing. Grandma,

Forever thankful to Grandma Litwiller.

although small in stature, would faithfully carry the accordion onto the bus and into the hospital for Janet to use. Once we arrived, she would set us in the middle of the hallway, and we'd sing our hearts out. One time she stood a fair distance away from where we were and said loudly, "Girls, sing 'How Great I Am!'" We laughed and said, "Grandma, we think you mean 'How Great Thou Art!'" We've had many chuckles over that.

One time we were even asked to sing at a funeral. Janet said later that she was scared spitless, but we must have done a good job because we kept getting requests to sing at different venues. Each time we sang, our confidence increased.

Can you recall a time that you were given a break, and something turned out well? It's always good to go back to your roots to see how far you've come. It's also good to be thankful for those "shoulders you stood on" to get where you are now.

Surrounding Grandma Litwiller in later years.

The Dubrick Family

Oh, sing to the LORD a new song! Sing to the LORD, all the earth. **Psalm 96:1**

After a couple of years, Daddy joined Janet and me and we became a trio. He played the guitar and sang tenor while Janet played the accordion and mostly sang alto. I usually sang soprano. I cannot recall how we learned harmony, but we each could slip into soprano, alto, or tenor with ease. The Dubrick Family became a reality.

We loved to harmonize in the car as we drove from venue to venue. We found it hilarious that when we sang a fast song, daddy would drive fast. When we sang a slow song, he'd drive really slowly and annoy the other drivers. It didn't matter though, because we were getting blessed in our car as we sang praises to God.

Our calendar seemed full most weekends. We were willing to go wherever we were invited, no matter how small the church or audience. The only drawback? Daddy did not have a good sense of direction and with no such thing as a GPS to guide us back then, each trip became an adventure. Mom and Dad would ask whoever they booked with for directions to the church. But they would ask friends and family for directions to the actual town.

One time, my Uncle Elmer said, "When you get to highway 15, stay straight all the way into the town."

Well, that sounded easy, right? It certainly should have been, except that the road curved to the left, and straight ahead was a gravel road. Daddy figured straight meant straight, so we ended up in a farmer's yard. He was quite upset that he was not told about the curve in the road!

We laugh about it today, but at the time it wasn't funny.

Sometimes my parents would calculate how much time it would take to get to the destination, and then they would add another hour of *get lost* time. No one even thought to laugh at this at the time, because arriving late was frowned upon.

Many a time, though, we'd be the first car in the parking lot waiting patiently for the janitor to unlock the doors of the venue. To

Daddy, it was worth being early to avoid the anxiety of being late! "Better to be an hour too soon than a minute too late."

Daddy was a smart cookie.

Did your family have a quirk or two? We all have them, including children. As kids, we don't see them as quirks, though. It's only as adults that we can look back and hopefully, smile. As parents, our kids will have the same memories of our silliness, but that goes with the territory.

Front Row Left to Right: Jane, Nancy
Back Row: Janet, Mom, Daddy.

New Style of Music

I will sing of mercy and justice; To You, O LORD, I will sing praises. **Psalm 101:1**

One weekend, my parents were invited to an "All Night Sing" concert at Massey Hall in Toronto. We had never heard of Southern Gospel music before and Daddy soon became enthralled with this new style. He figured it would suit our family trio perfectly, and indeed it did. They bought some vinyl records that evening in Toronto and were eager to find out where they could buy more.

Because the stores in our area did not carry Gospel music records, it was with great joy that Mom and Daddy discovered a late-night radio program on Sundays. Thrilled that the show aired many of their favourite Gospel groups, they put a plan in place. Although it might be considered illegal now, they did not feel they were doing anything wrong and would record the hour-long program on reel-to-reel tape. Each Monday morning, I would wake up, eager to hear the songs they had taped, wondering which ones we'd learn. Once we all agreed on the songs we liked best, two of us would begin the long process of getting the lyrics on paper. One would turn the tape player on and off. The other would write down the words. Often, we'd have to rewind it several times to understand them correctly. Even then we'd get some words wrong, but they were usually close enough.

With just lyrics in hand, we'd learn each one with Daddy and Janet playing their instruments by ear. Because Janet and I were young, we memorized the lyrics easily, but poor Daddy had a harder time and we'd have to practice often for his sake. He acknowledged this and would apologize, but no way were we going to use "cheat sheets" when we sang. That just wouldn't do!

With the old-style reel-to-reel tape recorders, once the tape finished it would continue to spin rapidly if no one shut it off. That would eat up pieces of the tape, so we needed to find a way to know when we had reached the end of the tape. We thought it would help if we asked four-year-old Jane to record a little ditty at the end of each reel in a sing-song voice: "This is the end of the tape—*boop,*

boop. This is the end of tape *boop, boop.* You can now turn it over or turn it off." That would be our cue to rush into the living room and press the stop button. I can still hear it today and that memory always makes me smile.

New technology is helpful, but sometimes it's nice to walk down memory lane and remember how it used to be.

There is a saying that talks about how we look at our past through rose-coloured glasses. That is probably true, but sometimes it causes us to sigh a bit at "the good old days." I often think of how one day I may look back on my life now, sigh, and wish for "the good old days." That is why it is important to make each day count and enjoy it to the fullest.

Four-Year-Old Jane

Train up a child in the way he should go, And when he is old he will not depart from it. **Proverbs 22:6**

Daddy, Janet, and I had been singing for about six months and always rehearsed in the living room. One evening, our four-year-old sister, Jane, sang along with us as she played with her toys. Instinctively, all three of us sang quieter, and as we listened, we were amazed at the quality and strength of her voice. Daddy then motioned for Janet and me to harmonize and let Jane take the lead while he dropped out. Much to our delight, Jane kept singing, and even with harmony on either side of her, she kept right on pitch. We were excited and proceeded to teach her to sing her first song, "I Woke Up This Morning Feeling Fine." There was one problem. With Jane only being four, she had to memorize the songs. After all, she could not read yet. She easily caught on and soon the Dubrick Family singing group was complete.

Back in the early 1960s, if a venue had a microphone, there would be only one, so for us all to be heard, we had to have Jane stand on a chair. We got a big kick out of watching an audience's reaction when they saw Jane sing for the first time. At the beginning, they thought it fascinating to see a cute little girl stand on a chair, but when Jane started to sing, the people would all have the same reaction. First, they were polite, but then they would nudge each other and point, then grin from ear to ear. In fact, Jane sometimes sang so loud that she could easily drown out both Janet and me. We had to ask her to tone it down every so often.

But things did not always go well. Because Jane was only four years old when she joined our group, there were times when she refused to sing. We would all be introduced, but if Jane didn't feel like singing, she wouldn't budge! Finally, when Janet made up our list of songs, she would create two—one with Jane in it and one without. We simply took it in stride, and soon she grew out of it and sang at every engagement.

We still have people coming up to us. "We remember when Jane stood on a chair to sing!" It must have been amazing, but, as carefree children, we took it all in stride. However, when we see any four-year-old sing now, we are impressed even more that Jane could sing with such power and quality at that age. When she grew older, we had to agree that she had the best voice of all of us. She accepted the accolades with grace.

None of us can take credit for our gifts. We must thank the Giver—God, the One who entrusted us with the ability to sing and perform at an early age. We are filled to overflowing with gratitude.

Never forget to thank God for the gifts He has given you. You may have had to work hard to perfect them, but rudimentary, God-given talent is a gift to celebrate.

Dressing up four-year-old Jane.

Family Ties

> *Therefore by Him let us continually offer the sacrifice of praise to God, that is, the fruit of our lips, giving thanks to His name.*
> **Hebrews 13:15**

It is heartwarming that both Mom and Daddy came from families with mothers who loved God and prayed for their family. They both enjoyed a good laugh which helped in difficult situations. As in every home, there were problems, but both my parent's mothers were the stabilizing influences in their lives. Interestingly enough, both my grandmothers were drawn to "the black sheep" when it came to choosing a spouse. Although I loved both my grandfathers, I know my grandmothers had their share of struggles with each of them.

Daddy had eight brothers and sisters, and Mom had seven siblings. I loved my aunts and uncles on both sides and always enjoyed visiting with them. No one needed an invitation or even to call ahead. We just showed up, whenever, at each other's homes.

Our home had a large recreation room in the basement, so many family gatherings were held there. Daddy and his brothers would sing and harmonize. They all had good voices and would sing songs like, "I want a gal just like the gal that married dear old dad" and "Dinah won't you blow your horn."

For all of us listening, it was like a little bit of Heaven, and I think we all hated when the show was over. We can honestly say, "A good time was had by all."

Each of the five brothers would lead with their arms and we loved to watch. How I wish we would have been able to record those songs back in the day, or even better yet, have it on video. But we only read about things like video watches and the like in Dick Tracy comic books back in the late 50s. Too bad.

My relatives on both sides were talented and many of them could play an instrument. Unfortunately, neither family had an outlet to perform, so their talents didn't see much action. We shall be forever grateful to our church and minister who first saw potential in Janet and me. Later, when Daddy and Jane joined Janet and me, we were all so appreciative to have been given ample opportunity to sing and begin our musical careers.

Here was a good reminder by American author, Dutch Sheets, that kept us grounded: "No matter how important our activities may be, including working for God, they don't trump the time with God."

Laughing Family

A merry heart does good, like medicine, ... **Proverbs 17:22a**

My first memories are of laughter. Relatives and friends would frequently gather at our home where hearty laughter filled the air. My mom loved to entertain and was an excellent cook, so that helped draw the crowds.

Our house did not have a formal dining room so if there were too many people to fit into the kitchen, mom would calmly set tables up in the living room. Nothing seemed to faze her, and she took everything in stride. I joyfully anticipated when company came knocking. Oh, if only those walls could talk!

The Dubricks and the Litwillers enjoyed visiting together and got along well. I found it interesting when one of my Aunts on Daddy's side said, "Nancy, you laugh just like our mother did." What makes it so intriguing is Grandma Dubrick died two years before I was born. It reveals yet again that we inherit parts of our personality and giftings from generations before us.

Daddy didn't like to go many places without us girls, but one time my Mom's sister, Doris, and her husband, Al, and Mom and Daddy, decided to go to Victoria Park to rent canoes. It was a beautiful park with a small lake and lots of ducks and geese. With that many fowl polluting the water, however, made it less than pleasant, so no swimming allowed. When the four of them arrived home that day, they were laughing, and Mom and Daddy were dripping wet. Apparently, they had tipped the canoe and had fallen into the dirty water. It hadn't been that deep, but they had to carry the canoe back to shore, bearing in mind the mucky doo-doo in the lake. Not pleasant! To add insult to injury, my parents were fined heavily for tipping the canoe. Daddy could hardly tell the story. Tears rolled down his cheeks as the others roared with laughter.

"I had to reach into my filthy, wet trousers to pull out my wallet and pay the fine with soggy bills." This story reinforced the fact that if a story lends itself to a good laugh, then by all means, share it.

Such stories cause me to pause when I realize that I am who I am partly because of my upbringing. I did not get to choose who my parents would be, what country I'd be born in, nor what century, but I am thankful for each blessing. I am humbled and ever so thankful that God orchestrated events so that Mom and Daddy would meet, marry, and have three daughters. I am blessed with talents that come from both sides of my family tree and can honestly say that the gift of laughter is at the top of the list. If we can laugh at ourselves and most situations, it lightens the load and helps us carry on.

Is laughter important to you? Are you able to see the lighter side of situations? Can you laugh at yourself? I've read that a good belly laugh is like an internal jog. We not only get to burn calories, but it cleanses our systems, too. Ask God to show you how to laugh, and I believe you'll feel much better for it.

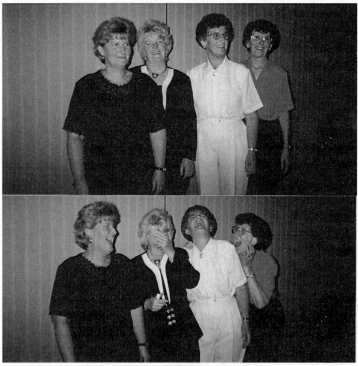

Mom and her sisters posing for a serious photo—but not for long.

Yukon or Bust

For God has not given us a spirit of fear, but of power and of love and of a sound mind. **2 Timothy 1:7**

Our singing family began to receive invitation after invitation to sing at churches in our area. The more we sang, the better known we became. Soon we found our musical talents in great demand. We worked hard to hone our craft, enjoying each performance, and all of us loved meeting new people.

One of the ministers from a little church nearby asked us if we would possibly consider going to the Yukon with him and his wife for six weeks in the summer of 1964. Pastor Don Hill had a cousin, Keith Parks, who lived in British Columbia (B.C.) and wanted us to be part of their evangelistic team to preach the gospel to the people in Northern B.C. and the Yukon. This was not an easy decision for my family for it meant that Daddy would have to take all that time off work without pay, and Janet would have to quit her job, hoping they'd rehire her when we returned.

After much prayer, we decided that we were supposed to go. Pastor Don and Pastor Keith would be the speakers and our family would be the singers. The church purchased and converted an old flat nose bus. Off we went in our new home on wheels, complete with shimmering, sky-blue paint and "Wings of Faith" written in big white letters on the side.

All went well for the first 100 miles into our journey. Then someone noticed smoke coming out of the engine. Daddy understood about cars, so he knew we had to get it checked out. Daddy pulled into a gas station so a mechanic could look at it.

"Your engine is toast. How far are you planning on going?" he asked, wiping his hands on a greasy rag.

"The Yukon." Daddy replied.

The mechanic laughed. "Good luck."

Daddy was determined though. He talked to the mechanic to confirm his suspicions. So, with Daddy's expertise, a lot of prayer, and by purchasing oil in five-gallon drums, we made it to the Yukon and back.

It seemed important to Daddy to visit that same gas station on our way home six weeks later. When we pulled in, the mechanic just stood there with his hands on his hips, pushed his hat back and said, "You didn't go all the way to the Yukon and back with that motor did you?" We smiled and assured him that yes, we did!

"God knew that He had a plan for us and kept that crippled motor running so we could tell hundreds of people about Jesus," Dad told him.

The mechanic shook his head in wonder as we pulled away, waving. I have so many memories of that trip.

I had forgotten about one funny memory, though, but Janet reminded me. And, in keeping with the oil theme—*Castrol Oil*, to be specific—it gave me a good giggle. At that time, it was apparently important to use the same oil in a vehicle. The mechanics used the brand, *Castrol Oil*, but it wasn't always easy to find along the journey. One time, Daddy went into a gas station to ask if they had any *Castrol Oil*. The mechanic looked at him funny and said, "Sir, this is a gas station. You need to go to a drug store for castor oil." Janet remembers Daddy coming back into the bus laughing about the mix-up.

We carried on and continued to sing our little hearts out. Along the way we were invited to a rural television station to sing. Keith and his wife Anita, had previously driven the Alaska Highway to scope places out and make arrangements for where we would minister. This rural television station was one of the contacts. Fascination gripped us as we realized the resourcefulness of sound engineers and other staff. They had used egg cartons to soundproof the studio. How ingenious.

The Alaska highway, built during the war, remained unpaved in 1964. It made for a bumpy ride; potholes that lasted for hundreds of miles; no guardrails on the snaking highway. Treacherous curves at the base of the mountains. Every few miles, we would notice crosses standing at the side of the road, indicators of how many had been killed at certain locations. This warning revealed to all who drove on this road that this wasn't a walk in the park, but a very dangerous undertaking. Travelling those roads in a huge bus did not lessen the danger. It made it worse. The men took turns driving white knuckling it the whole way. However, we made it home safe and sound with lots of stories to tell. Only eternity will reveal those souls who came to Christ because of our ministry in the Yukon. I do hope I get the chance to sit down with them in Heaven someday to hear their story.

Do you have some unique trips that you could share with your friends or family? It doesn't have to be to the Yukon. Even a simple camping trip can yield countless tales. Any time we step out of our comfort zone it can yield numerous stories. Be brave and recount them all.

Not a Good Year

> *My brethren, count it all joy when you fall into various trials, knowing that the testing of your faith produces patience. But let patience have its perfect work, that you may be perfect and complete, lacking nothing.* **James 1:2-4**

Not all of life is a wonderful adventure. I could not admit what I am about to share here, for most of my life. But now I feel the time is right.

I failed not just one, but two grades. Grades four and seven. All my friends moved on to another grade and I was left behind feeling great shame. I didn't think I could ever share my pain with anyone, so I buried it deep. Even as I write these words, tears well.

During my second time in grade seven, the school board built a brand new Senior Public School. The new school, located a mile and a half away from our house, was for grade seven and eight students. It was no fun each morning when I had to walk past my old school.

I must admit, though, that it felt cool to have a locker and to walk from class to class. My fellow students elected me as class president. While in grade seven, I entered a public speaking contest in our school. I won. My win meant I would move to the next level. How excited I felt to be presenting my speech again at a Kitchener Legion. My joy was doubled when I won again, too!

I had the advantage because of my experience being on stage for so many years. I was no stranger to performing in front of a crowd. Why couldn't school have been that easy?

December of that same year brought tragedy into our family. It was a regular school morning on December 17th, 1964. My home room teacher held up a mitten.

"Does this belong to anyone?" he asked. Innocently, I put my hand up.

"Nancy, you have a detention for leaving your mitten in the hallway." This stunned me, and I blurted out, "But sir, it must have fallen out of my locker and I didn't notice." I thought my explanation would change his mind, but nope, the detention remained. After the detention, mom had to pick me up because by the time my detention was over, it was dark and cold, not to mention, a long walk home.

Little did I know how trivial my detention would soon seem. When I arrived home Daddy was still there, which was unusual. Daddy's profession as a tool-and-die maker, often required him to work nights which meant he had to leave before we got home from school. What a surprise it was that day seeing Daddy still there when I arrived home, even if I was a little later than usual. The thought came, "Oh no, Daddy's not going to work so that means we'll have to spend the evening rehearsing."

Instead, Daddy said, "I never get to see you girls when I work nights, so I thought I'd wait to see you all together." He had never been late for work in his life, but he would have been that night.

We were totally unaware that we would never see our daddy alive again. At 10:00 p.m. that evening, he dropped dead from a massive heart attack.

He was 39.

We all have had tragedy in our lives. No one seems to escape the harsh realities of life. One good thing that comes from difficulties is that we can honestly say to someone who is hurting, "I've been where you are. I know how it feels to go through deep heartache and trials." Sometimes that is all it takes for the other person to know they are not alone.

The Funeral

The LORD is gracious and full of compassion, Slow to anger and great in mercy. The LORD is good to all, And His tender mercies are over all His works. **Psalm 145:8-9**

Of course, our family was in shock. We knew Daddy had a heart condition, but he seemed fine when we saw him before he left for work hours earlier. Mom had suddenly become a widow at 37, with three girls at home, ages 17, 14, and eight.

Mom had to buy a black suit to wear to the funeral. All three girls went with Mom to help her find something suitable. I wanted to cry to the saleslady, "My daddy just died. This suit is for our mother to wear to his funeral" but I stayed quiet because I didn't want to make any waves. Mom showed us how to be strong, so we did our best to follow her example.

Walking into the funeral home for the first time and seeing Daddy in the casket tore at my heart. I did not want to see my daddy in the casket. I hated it and desperately wanted it to be a dream that I would surely wake up from. Sadly, the truth hit me hard. He had, indeed, left us.

At the funeral home, Mom ended up comforting many of those who came. "He was so young!" This became the mantra of those who lined up to pay their respects. I remember thinking, "He was 39!" I wasn't being disrespectful, but to a 14-year-old, 39 was getting up there.

Mom's positive attitude shone each time she talked about how she knew her young husband was with Jesus. She showed us, by example, that although we would miss our daddy terribly, we would find the strength and would make it on our own, all the while constantly reassuring us that someday we would see him again in heaven.

Our family was well-known in the community, so the church was packed for the funeral. We asked The Sharon Gospel Singers to sing in the service because Daddy enjoyed the music of these four sisters. We had often sung at the same concerts, so it seemed right to have them there. After the funeral, we found out they had never sung at a celebration of life before, but we were thankful that they agreed. Daddy would have approved.

Not long after we said goodbye to Daddy, we changed our stage name from The Dubrick Family to The Dubrick Sisters. The first song we sang in public after Daddy died, "I Know Who Holds Tomorrow[2]," tugged at everyone's emotions. The song speaks about how we sure do not know the future and how, even though we don't understand why things happen, we do know Who holds the future. There was not a dry eye in the place.

Even though Mom was far too young to be left with three girls at home, her strength and courage carried us through, and our busy lives continued.

Strange how some things will be forever etched in my memory. I learned because of what my parents taught me at an early age, never to fear death, for it would be like falling asleep on earth and waking up in heaven. Daddy just made it there ahead of us.

One of Daddy's sisters thought my mother wasn't grieving enough. "But Evelyn, Wilf is home safe," my mother would say.

That was the way she coped with her loss, so we learned from her example to see death as simply going home.

Do you have that assurance? It is only because of Jesus' sacrifice on the cross that we will enter into that heavenly place. All we have to do is accept the gift of salvation and to know without a shadow of a doubt that we will someday see Jesus face to face. How glorious that will be.

---

[2] I Know Who Holds Tomorrow; ©1950; Ira Stanphill (1914-1993)

More Trials Ahead

In the multitude of my anxieties within me, Your comforts delight my soul. **Psalm 94:19**

Barely three months after Daddy's death, Janet and I were involved in a serious car accident. We had been singing at a little church in Rosebank and had invited friends to come to our house for juice and cookies after the evening service. Our friends offered Janet and me a ride home. Mom and Jane had gone on ahead of us to get things ready.

I don't remember a lot because it all happened so quickly. I had been sitting in the front seat of the vehicle and was suddenly thrown headfirst through the windshield. We had apparently hit a parked car. Back in the 60s most cars did not have seatbelts, and if they did, few people wore them, including me. Janet wasn't hurt as much because she sat in the back seat. When Janet tried to help me out of the car, she paled when she saw my face covered in blood. The crash had alerted the family in the home across from the scene. They rushed to the door. That's when Janet yelled, asking if we could use their phone to call the police. She did and then immediately called Mom. Mom knew something bad had happened because of Janet's shaky voice. She quickly got in the car and drove to the site, arriving just as they were taking me to the ambulance.

The policeman looked my way as they were carrying me out on the stretcher. "I don't think that one will make it," he said.

The medical team immediately whisked me into surgery. Forty-two stitches later, I came out of recovery and it was clear I would make it after all. After surgery, the doctor sat with my mother.

"Mrs. Dubrick, I did my best, but plastic surgery can do wonders." I can't imagine how Mom must have felt to hear the news of the accident, to rush to the scene, to hear the policeman's solemn prediction, and later to hear the surgeon's bittersweet words.

I will never forget how kind the nurses were to me. After the accident, my long hair became a tangled, matted mess filled with dried blood. The nurses kept a towel covering my head until, a few days after my accident, a sweet nun brought bottles of warmed distilled water and invited me to sit in a chair. She invited me to tip my head back with a basin underneath. She was going to wash my hair. She poured bottle after bottle over my hair. The stench of the dried blood was overpowering, yet she didn't leave me until the water eventually ran clear. Very gently, so as not to disturb the many stitches, she patiently combed my hair until all the tangles were out. I am emotional even now as I recall her kindness to me that day. When I get to heaven, I want to be able to tell her how I never forgot her kindness. How when she was a loving servant to a 14-year-old girl who survived a motor vehicle accident a few months after her daddy died. She is surely reaping the reward for her patience and love.

Thankfully, the policeman's prediction turned out to be wrong. Unless you look closely, it's hard to tell where the stitches were. Even without plastic surgery. I do have a small piece of bone out of my left eyebrow, but rarely anyone notices. God was my plastic surgeon and I praised him for healing me.

We all have questions about why God allows certain tragedies into our lives. Sometimes we see a reason, but other times we must just say, "Father, I don't understand, but it is enough that You do."

If you are struggling with a bad memory, whether they happened yesterday or decades ago, let it go. No matter how hard you try or want it to be different, you cannot undo what has already happened. It benefits both your body and soul when you can finally say, "All is well," and leave it in God's hands. You'll most likely feel better when you do this. The burden will lift, and you will be able to face the next trial without carrying the burdens of the past.

Funny Dubrick Sisters' Stories

You will show me the path of life; In Your presence is fullness of joy; At Your right hand are pleasures forevermore. **Psalm 16:11**

Anyone who has been on stage knows that strange things can happen. Sometimes they are embarrassing. Sometimes they are funny. Sometimes they are both!

We were the special singers at our church camp in the summer of 1965. As always, we sat in the front pew near the platform. We were called up to sing and then right after we had finished, we headed back to our seats to listen to the sermon. Unfortunately, the venue lacked air conditioning and even with the windows wide open, the air became stifling. Eight-year-old Jane sat between Janet and me. Soon, she grew tired. She laid her head on Janet's lap and her feet on mine and soon fell fast asleep. We thought nothing of it until Jane started to make funny noises. Janet and I were beside ourselves, trying to hold back the laughter. We had just settled down when Jane would make the noise again, and this time we couldn't win for losing. Not too sure if anyone else heard it, but to us, it sounded as if we had brought the microphone down with us to the pew.

Another time, we were in a rather conservative church. We were used to performing in a more relaxed atmosphere, so we were probably a bit uptight to begin with.

Mom made most of our outfits, so we were always dressed alike. Sometimes we wore a flower in our lapels and once we had a carnation at our waists. With some of our dresses we wore pearl necklaces. Like on this particular day.

I was fiddling with my pearls as we waited in the pew. Suddenly, the string broke and the pearls went down the front of my dress. I prayed that there would be one more congregational song before we would be called up to sing, but it wasn't to be.

"We now call The Dubrick Sisters up to sing."

My heart sank.

I had no choice but to stand and walk to the platform. This church did not have carpet, but the "ping, ping, ping" of the pearls dropping and bouncing on the hardwood floor, echoed throughout the sanctuary. We said nothing, but the pearls kept dropping and my face got redder and redder.

If it was later in our career, we would likely have told the congregation what happened and given everyone a laugh, but back then we didn't have the courage to say anything. I think some hidden ones were still ping, ping, pinging on the way down again. We laughed about it after, but oh, the humiliation! The poor custodian must have wondered that day who cast the pearls all over the sanctuary (and why)!

For a while Mom would put Jane's hair up into a Pebbles Flintstones high-ponytail style, and it looked adorable on her. One time we were invited to an old church that had beautiful stained-glass windows at the back. Again, we were in the front pew waiting to be called up to sing. The sun shone behind Jane. Janet and I noticed that her shadow made her hairdo look like a fountain on top of her head. Try as we may, we couldn't stop laughing at the caricature on the wall. Soon Jane saw it too. We laughed as quietly as we could. But people were looking at us, so it must have been evident that something had tickled our funny bones. No matter which way Jane turned, the fountain shadow remained. It was with great relief when we were finally called up to sing. By the time we returned to our seats the sun had moved just enough that the shadow had disappeared, thank goodness.

All the way home we roared just thinking of it. Jane never wanted her hair to be put up like that again and we all agreed that it was probably for the best.

Laughter is healing, but it can also be embarrassing. There is a time to laugh and a time to be serious, but when something hits our funny bone, it can be difficult to keep the laughter at bay. May as well enjoy the moment and get it over with!

High School Days

*"Blessed are the poor in spirit,
For theirs is the kingdom of heaven.* **Matt. 5:3**

After grade seven, I was informed that it would be a good idea for me to skip grade eight and enroll in a two-year program at the downtown high school. I jumped at the opportunity. This meant I would not be walking to the high school closer to home where my sister, Janet, attended. Instead, I eagerly took the bus each morning to my new school.

I knew no one at this school and I felt intimidated at first. However, I must have gained popularity for once again, I was voted class president. This meant I had to be on a committee that convened just after school hours.

At my first committee meeting, when I stated my class as 2F, a member of the committee announced that I was in a lowly two-year course, rather than a four or five-year course. My face burned red from humiliation and I wanted to flee. I had no choice but to take my place at the table with the others. I did not say one word the entire time. The intimidation returned and our interactions were awkward.

Much to my surprise though, my grades didn't suffer with marks being in the high 90s on every exam. I thoroughly enjoyed home economics and typing became my favourite class. It didn't take long before I caught on and I started hitting those keys on the old-fashioned typewriter correctly every time. The first time I typed on an electric typewriter I thought it a dream.

I never got involved in after-school activities and now I wish I had. The school had an excellent drama coach who led first class theatrical productions, but I lacked the self-confidence to even audition. It was one of those missed opportunities that I regret, but there was no going back.

I'm sure I am not alone in wishing I would have expanded my horizons more in my youth. I like this quote from Mark Batterson from his book, *The Grave Robber*: "God has given us a free will, but no one orchestrates opportunities like the Omnipotent One. He provides an entry ramp into every opportunity and an exit ramp out of every temptation."

God gives us choices and never forces anything on us. Every experience can be used for our benefit.

Believing Lies

Blessed is the man who trusts in the LORD, And whose hope is the LORD. **Jeremiah 17:7**

"Nancy, please come into my office right after your last class." I was in grade 10 at the time when I received the message from my guidance counsellor. I had never been summoned like this before and wondered what I'd done wrong. The counsellor sat behind his desk and welcomed me in. After some small talk, he leaned toward me and said, "What the *h###* are you doing in this course?"

I was taken aback. I wasn't used to hearing anyone swear, especially not a teacher. Confusion set in, initially.

"What do you mean?" I asked.

"Nancy, you do not belong here. It's evident that this two-year program content is far below your ability. Why did you choose a two-year course instead of a four-year course?"

"Because I'm stupid!" He sat back in his chair and softly asked, "Who told you that?" Now it was my turn to sit back in my chair.

"I just know I'm stupid. I failed two grades before I came here, and I can't wait to graduate and begin working and earning a wage."

The poor guidance counsellor tried to convince me that I wasn't stupid and that I should transfer into the regular four-year course. But my mind was made up. Convinced that I would never be able to keep up, I emphasized my reluctance to even consider changing programs. I had trouble wondering how he thought I could manage. Nothing he, or anyone could say would change how stupid I still felt.

I'm sure my counsellor just shook his head when I walked out of his office that day. In my mind, I pretty much figured that he did not know what he was talking about. Why did he think I didn't belong in the two-year program, anyway? I was baffled. Oh, the lies we believe. When it came time to graduate, that same teacher asked me to give the Valedictorian speech which I did with ease.

I am ever so thankful that my husband is my cheerleader. Whenever I feel stupid, his answer is, "I would never have married a stupid woman!" Because of his faith in me, and encouragement from others, I have been able to excel in many different areas and would eventually become a published author. How I wish that guidance counsellor could see what I have accomplished. I like to believe that he wouldn't be the least bit surprised.

What lies have you believed? Perhaps you were put down as a child by parents, relatives, or friends. Perhaps you had potential but could not get past those voices in your head, whispering lies about who you were and what you could or could not do. Ask God to show you the lies and to reveal His truth to you. He created you after all, so He knows you best. God is more than willing to point out the lies so you can become all He intended for you to be.

A Ventriloquist is Born

> *Therefore humble yourselves under the mighty hand of God, that He may exalt you in due time, casting all your care upon Him, for He cares for you.* **1 Peter 5:6-7**

During my teenage years, I taught myself how to be a ventriloquist, thanks to My Uncle Len. He had purchased "Jerry" at a second-hand store in Batavia, New York in the early 1950s. Jerry, who became my very first ventriloquist doll, had a broken string that controlled how his mouth opened. But Uncle Len fixed it and would bring Jerry out occasionally to do a little performance. As children, we were mesmerized. Uncle Len was no ventriloquist and moved his lips, but we didn't care!

By the time I turned 15, my mom, Janet, and I, along with Aunt Doris and Uncle Elmer, were entertaining and teaching children all over Ontario. We knew that Jerry would be a huge hit, so we asked if Uncle Len could come along. He said he couldn't, but he looked at me and said, "Nancy, if you can teach yourself how to be a ventriloquist, you can have him."

"Really?"

So, I did! I learned how to substitute letters (you can't say B, M, P, or W without moving your lips). I practised hard until I was able to coordinate and synchronize Jerry's mouth every time there was a syllable. Before long, I mastered it, and we were right, Jerry became a huge hit.

That same year, I was thrilled to learn that our school had a talent show. My hand went up right away. The evening of the show, when I walked on stage with Jerry, everyone loved him. Later my homeroom teacher told me about how he had been sitting with another teacher at the time.

"Man, I sure wouldn't want to have her in my class. Can you imagine the tricks she could play on everyone else?" My teacher said he slid down in his seat and admitted, "I have her for home room." The other teacher offered his sympathies and we laughed at my teacher's "bad luck."

At our first week-long children's meeting, in a little church in Northern Ontario, I told Jerry on the final day that we'd be leaving, and he felt sad. He said he'd miss the kids and then said, "What a pity!" Now, to everyone else, it sounded like "pity," but my sisters and cousins knew differently and began laughing. In order to say "P," a ventriloquist must substitute the softer version of the letter "T." From then on, Jerry would say, "What a shame!"

Since then, Jerry has travelled to many countries around the world. Little did Uncle Len or I know the ramifications of him finding Jerry in that second-hand store and deciding to entrust him to me. God knew of course, and I think He just smiled when Uncle Len found Jerry at that second-hand store, and when he gave Jerry to me years later. Indeed, Jerry has been with me for over five decades and I can't imagine my life without this cute little guy.

What seemed a small kindness at the time has turned into huge opportunities. Never dismiss small beginnings. Remember that the mighty oak started from a single seed.

Jerry and me in our first promotional photo.

First Job

He who heeds the word wisely will find good, And whoever trusts in the LORD, happy is he. **Proverbs 16:20**

Right after graduation from high school, I earnestly began to look for a job and was thrilled to land one at our area Real Estate Board. Not only did I love my job, but the office was within easy walking distance of our home. My responsibilities included typing the listings, developing negatives, printing the listings, and mailing them to Realtors. I enjoyed my job immensely. I couldn't believe when I received my first paycheque—a whole $50.00 a week. I gave Mom $25.00 and that left me about $18.00 each week after taxes. I felt like the richest person alive. I tithed 10% to God, saved some for the future, and the rest was pocket money.

Once a month a handsome young man would come and service the huge printer at the office. I looked forward to these times because we laughed a lot together. I like to think I would have been one of his favourite customers. Wishful thinking? Maybe, maybe not. But I sure looked forward to seeing him once a month.

One day during my handsome service friend's regular visit, my boss decided to come in and correct me harshly for something I'd done. I endured her tirade but felt relieved when the serviceman left, although I dreaded his next visit. I was sure that he must have been thinking how much of a loser I was. I recall shrinking when he walked in a month later. I expected him to shun me. But his first words shocked me. In a whisper he said, "Man, you sure have a witch for a boss don't you!" It took me a while to realize that he was talking about my boss and not me. After all, she did not have to chide me in front of him. It could have waited. Relief flooded through my whole being. He still liked me!

That experience taught me a huge life lesson. Whenever we put someone down in front of another person it does not make the victim look bad, it makes the perpetrator look worse. Little did my boss know what she taught me with that lecture. Why she felt she had to do it then is beyond me. I felt horrible for one whole month, but the true lesson lasted for the rest of my life.

There's a good quote that says, "Be slow to speak and quick to listen." Great advice. It is far easier to swallow a harsh retort than to try and gobble it back into one's mouth after it has been spoken. I've also found that it's not a tasty treat to have my foot in my mouth. How much better to refrain from spewing ugly words, than having them hanging out there for the world to see.

Being Miss Nancy

Let no one despise your youth, but be an example to the believers in word, in conduct, in love, in spirit, in faith, in purity. **1 Tim 4:12**

When the time came for me to take over the Junior Church responsibilities from my Aunt Doris, it filled my heart with joy. Jerry called me Miss Nancy and the children followed suit. The children would be in the service upstairs until time for the sermon, and then they would come down to me. I'd have songs, Bible memory verses, object lessons, Bible stories with beautiful flannelgraph on gorgeous backgrounds, or illustrated stories. The children were always thrilled whenever Jerry would make an appearance. I worked hard coming up with new skits. I found some ventriloquist books, but just used the outline and turned them into skits that I thought were better for my purpose. I realized I thoroughly enjoyed putting my own spin on these skits and the children rewarded me with their hearty approval.

I'd often buy materials from popular Christian companies with my own money or hand copy whatever my Aunt Doris made. Working on projects all week caused me to come alive and I eagerly looked forward to Sundays. I am not sure how many in the congregation realized I was in the basement teaching the children, but that didn't matter. I knew this was where God wanted me to be. What an honour.

Decades later at the funeral of our former beloved Pastor Shrier, many of my former students returned to honour this great man of God. I got a real kick out of seeing some of the young people who'd moved away and heard some even admit that they had a terrible crush on Miss Nancy in Junior Church. This shocked me, but then I thought about some of the pictures of me when I was in my late teens and early 20s. I had to admit, I was a bit of a looker. At the time though, I had no idea that these boys liked me that much. Perhaps it turned out for the best. I was innocent in the male department and did not realize what might have been transpiring in their adolescent minds. (I *was* tickled pink though to think that several had a crush on me.)

I love the little verse from a CT Studd poem that says, "Only one life will soon be past. Only what's done for Christ will last." Each one of us has to make many choices every day. Do we go our own way and do our own thing, or do we sincerely ask God to direct our steps? I am thankful that even if we do mess up, God will pick us up, dust us off, and give us a clean slate to carry on if we ask Him. God has a plan for all of us, and He will reveal it one step at a time if we listen.

Another promotional photo with Jerry five years later. (Other than a new suit, he hasn't changed. But I have!)

Home is Where the Heart Is

For every house is built by someone, but He who built all things is God. **Hebrews 3:4**

Life continued to be good. Janet and I both worked fulltime so we could help pay the bills. We wanted to keep our mother in her home as long as possible for we knew she was content to be there. Mom kept herself busy with her Women's Missionary Society (WMS) work from church. She would spend countless hours artfully repurposing greeting cards, pasting them on heavy construction paper with Bible verses, and putting a pretty ribbon on top in order for the recipients to hang them on their walls. One of the parishioners of our church owned a thriving printing company and happily donated all the paper products she needed. The Canadian Bible Society supplied Bible verses in many languages. Mom sent thousands of cards to an organization where they were distributed to different countries. I wouldn't be surprised if there are still many of those gems on walls in homes around the world. Each one, a thing of beauty, and we were proud of her artistic skills.

We three girls were still singing as The Dubrick Sisters and had many engagements all over our area. We loved singing and travelling on weekends to various churches or organizations. I usually brought Jerry out, much to the delight of audiences.

Soon though, it became apparent that Mom needed to find a job, so she applied to work at a local long-term seniors' facility not too far from our home. She loved to tell this funny story about herself:

"I had been out of the workforce for almost 20 years and felt terribly nervous when I filled out the application for a job. Shortly after, I received a call asking me to come in for an interview. I dressed carefully for I wanted to make a good first impression. The interview seemed to go well and just before we said our goodbyes, the manager said she would let me know if I got the job. Relieved it was over, I drove to my sister Doris' home for a calming cup of tea. I kicked my shoes off at the door and we had a lovely visit. When the time came to leave, I couldn't believe my eyes. There on the landing of Doris' home, were two different shoes—both mine. One brown, the other black. One had a square toe and the other had a round toe. I screamed at first and then began to laugh. Doris wondered what could be so funny. I could only point to the two different shoes. All I could think about was what the manager must have thought about this kook who couldn't even dress herself and figured I'd never get hired. The next day however, I got called back into the office and the same manager said I had the job. I thanked her and got up to leave. At the door I turned around and said, "By the way, did you notice my shoes yesterday?" The manager said she hadn't, so I had no choice but to share with her my faux pas. We both had a good laugh."

Mom and her Siblings.
Front Row Left to Right: Gloria, Grandma, Ron.
Back Row Left to Right: Stan, Len, Mom, Doris, Joyce.

Mom loved that job and the residents adored her. She worked there for quite a while until a different opportunity came along.

Whenever we "lay an egg" we may as well get it out in the open so everyone can admire it. We all make mistakes. No one is exempt, so we may as well give everyone a good laugh. Mom got a kick out of sharing about her job interview. It never failed to get a good chuckle. Mom always thought the manager liked her even better after her confession, and they got along famously.

Wedding in the Family

And now abide faith, hope, love, these three; but the greatest of these is love. **1 Corinthians 13:13**

We knew, eventually, our family dynamics would change, and that change would come about when my sister, Janet, met her future husband, Hank. The sparks flew and soon it became evident that these two were made for each other.

Hank was a young boy when his father, mother, and younger brother, Klaus, emigrated from Germany to Canada. Their father's brother arrived first, claiming Canada was a land flowing with milk and honey. He offered to sponsor them, so it was easy for them to make the decision to come. Hank still remembers the long ocean voyage and the difference between Canadian and German cultures. The family had to learn English and lived in a couple of cramped rooms on their uncle's farm. The family was sorry they left their home country and quickly realized that Canada was not the land of milk and honey; only backbreaking work and toil.

Eventually they moved to Kitchener and began attending our church. Even before Hank and Janet began dating, my mom befriended Hank's mother and felt sorry for this German lady who seemed to be struggling with the language and culture. One day Mom felt impressed to put together a food box for this family and added things from our own cupboard. This was the first year of widowhood for Mom, yet she gave what she could and delivered the box. When Mrs. Sonnenberg carefully took everything out of the box, she broke down and cried.

"Onions! I had run out of onions and prayed for provision. God, you know a German cook must have onions and I ask that You give me some." Mom had no idea this prayer had been uttered but obeyed the little nudge to put some onions in the box. It brought hope back into this family's heart. God even cared about onions.

Before we knew it, there was a wedding to prepare for and, although happy for Janet, we still felt a huge loss at the thought of her leaving our nest. The "us four and no more" no longer applied. Soon the day dawned bright and clear. Janet made a beautiful bride and Hank, a handsome groom. I remember feeling sad when we went home to a house without Janet. Indeed, it took quite a while to get used to just the three of us, but Hank and Janet were over the moon in love.

We did visit back and forth of course, but I can still feel the longing I had for the "good old days." We continued to sing, but it grew more and more difficult to find dates that worked for us all and we began to turn down engagements. However, God had a plan for Mom, Jane, and me in the wings.

Have you had changes in your life that didn't exactly sit well? We can get so comfortable with routines that when a situation changes it can be upsetting. I get irritated sometimes just thinking about it. The key is to not mourn what is gone, but to look forward to what is ahead. It certainly helps with the loss.

1969. Janet as a beautiful bride with Jane and me as bridesmaids.

New Opportunity

Therefore do not be unwise, but understand what the will of the Lord is. **Ephesians 5:17**

I'd been working at the Real Estate Board for about three years, while Mom had been employed for about 18 months at the seniors' long-term care. Out of the blue, two job opportunities opened up for both of us. The husband of a long-time friend of my mom's called from Sarnia to tell us he needed help at his elegant motel. He knew that Mom was a widow with two girls at home. It meant relocating. But as an incentive, we were offered an apartment behind the office, free of charge, which sweetened the deal. I would be the receptionist and mom would work in the laundry with her friend's sister. My sister Jane would go to high school there and a bus would pick her up every morning. The more we talked about it, the better it sounded. We would make better money plus we could live rent-free and mom could rent our house to Hank and Janet. This seemed like the answer.

We made the move and attended the same church as Mom's friends and I soon became the Junior Church leader. The children there loved Jerry and I loved teaching them. The lovely motel had an indoor swimming pool in the center of the courtyard, and I'd hold pool parties occasionally for my young charges. After swimming, we'd go to the party room where we would enjoy snacks and play games.

Years later a woman told me how much of an impact I had on the lives of her children. "Those pool parties were a highlight and they still talk about it."

There was one fly in the ointment. I always worked the evening shift, 5:00 pm to midnight. Most of my new friends worked or went to school during the day and were free at night. There were some good times, but loneliness set in and I began eating out of boredom. Junk food, freely available in the lobby, tempted me far too often. My weight began to balloon.

After about a year, I'd had enough and contacted my friend, Karen, who worked at the University of Waterloo. I asked if she knew of any job openings her way. She shared an apartment near the university with three other girls and one of them was moving out. Perfect timing.

I quit my job at the motel and moved back to Waterloo after I landed a good position at the University. I shared a small office with two other girls, thrilled to have regular hours again. I lost the excess weight and felt much better. Karen and I were like two peas in a pod, sharing secrets, our non-existent love lives, and we laughed a lot.

Neither of us had a date on our first New Year's Eve together, but we decided to dress up anyway and go to the service at our church. It was usually a packed house with top notch entertainment.

"You stay by the door Nancy and I'll come and get you," Karen dished out her orders as the heavy snow fell.

Fair enough! I stood there, daydreaming about how my knight in shining armour was coming to get me. Then Karen pulled up, rolled down her window and yelled, "Need a ride lady?" My bubble burst but we laughed all the way to church.

Our apartment, always a hub of activity, had a poster board attached to the door so everyone who entered could sign it. The huge surface soon became full of names and cute sayings. Somehow, though, much to our disappointment, it disappeared. Oh, the stories that board could tell. We mourned its loss.

It's interesting from time to time to look back over our lives and see what different "roads" we took. Sometimes we are at a crossroad and must decide which way to take. Sometimes a road seems a good and profitable one to take and other times it seems like we goofed. However, God never takes His eyes off us and even if we've made a bad decision, He can turn it into good.

Enter David Seiling

Trust in the LORD with all your heart, And lean not on your own understanding; In all your ways acknowledge Him, And He shall direct your paths. **Proverbs 3:5-6**

While living in the apartment with three other gals, I received a phone call from David Seiling. David and I had known each other all our lives. We attended the same church in Kitchener up until we were about five years old. His family moved away but we'd still see each other from time to time. David and his brothers also sang while their mother accompanied them on the piano. I was delighted to hear from David and agreed to a date. I took careful thought of what to wear and my apartment mates sent me off on my adventure. I had a wonderful time at a company banquet where David worked, and we laughed a lot. Most of the time he talked about bicycling 3500 miles with a group called deCycles directed by Bob Hardley and his wife Dory. Little did I know the tremendous influence Bob and the deCycles would have on the lives of so many of my family (including having them as the honour guard at our wedding). But I am getting ahead of myself here. David had dozens of stories to tell that evening and it enthralled me. At the end of our date, he walked me to my door. We said our goodbyes and I slipped inside.

"Did you have a good time?" The girls grilled me. I assured them that I had had a wonderful time and answered a resounding "yes" when they asked if I'd go out with David Seiling again.

Naturally, I expected a second date. After all, we got along famously, and I eagerly wanted to see him again. One week passed and no phone call. Then two weeks, then two months with nary a peep. When the girls questioned me about the "no calls," I shrugged.

"Well, I'm just as puzzled as you are. I had a great time, but apparently he didn't." It disappointed me of course but life went on. What I didn't realize was that David went on two dates a year whether he needed them or not. He knew some friends who were womanizers, and he did not want that reputation. I happened to be his second date that year.

Sometimes communication is lacking and can cause quite a bit of confusion. However, as we look back, it usually works out for the better. At least we can have a cute story to share, and that's a good thing.

This Guy knows how to pack!
From Bottom to Top: Guitar case, sleeping bag, heavy coat, 10-speed bike, bicycle frame, duffle bag with clothes, and front and rear bicycle wheels.

Second Date

> *For by grace you have been saved through faith, and that not of yourselves; it is the gift of God, not of works, lest anyone should boast.* **Ephesians 2:8-9**

The more time passed, the more I doubted the good time David must have had on our date. When he finally got around to calling me for a second date, eight months later, my heart skipped a beat. I had a problem, though. "I'd love to go out with you David, but I am booked for an engagement with Jerry for a church dinner at a town hall." Things went quiet for a minute.

"But you can come along if you'd like," I told him. He agreed, and we drove to the venue together. Before my presentation, as we were sitting at the table eating, I thought of something.

"Did you bring your guitar with you?" I knew David played guitar. My mind raced when he said yes. I sang the simple tune to a little "duet" that Jerry and I always sang. David picked it up right away and did a fabulous job playing it for us on the guitar. I vividly recall thinking to myself when we walked to the curtained wings of the large stage, "That's the man I'm going to marry."

After that, David came along for most of my engagements and soon took part in every program that he could manage. We worked well together, and he had enough talent and experience on stage to fit right in. We were a match made in Heaven, but I had to convince him of that first!

Sometimes men take a little longer to understand the emotional part of a relationship. I knew that I loved David way before he realized he loved me. Have you ever had a similar experience? It can make for funny stories. Dig a few up and have a smile or two.

The Joyful Sound

Blessed are the people who know the joyful sound! They walk, O LORD, in the light of Your countenance. **Psalm 89:15**

Soon I became a part of a new and exciting singing group formed by some talented members of our church. We were called The Joyful Sound. Hank and Janet were already part of it, so I slipped in easily. The band did have a good and joyful sound, but we needed a bass player. David auditioned and they hired him immediately. Because we were the only singles in the group that meant we were paired off. This thrilled me! David still played it cool though and it bewildered (annoyed) me. I had my share of handsome suitors, so why wasn't he interested? This went on for quite a while until I thought the only way I would get his attention would be to accept a date from another guy and make sure he knew about it.

Although I am embarrassed about it now, I resorted to desperate measures. A young man I barely knew asked me out for lunch after church. I sweetly told him that I would love to go but had to be back right after for a Joyful Sound rehearsal. He agreed. After lunch he drove me to the church, and I invited him to come in to meet the band. I kept an eye out for David's reaction, but he didn't seem to notice. However, my plan worked and right after that he asked me on a real date without the Joyful Sound. I wonder whatever became of that young man. I never saw him again. Either he did not have a good time, or he saw through my ruse. Young man, wherever you are, please forgive me.

Sometimes desperate times call for desperate measures. Getting David to date me was one of them. I'm still a bit miffed that it took him so long to realize he almost missed out on a good catch. One thing you could say about David—he wasn't impulsive.

Have you ever had to do something a little out of the box to get someone's attention? Does it make you smile, or is it embarrassing? How did it turn out?

The Joyful Sound
Left to right: Ron Kechnie, Jane Dubrick, Janet and Hank Sonnenberg, Jim Todd, Nancy and David Seiling, Bernie Talbot.

Romantic Engagement

Now faith is the substance of things hoped for, the evidence of things not seen. **Hebrews 11:1**

David and I began dating regularly. Soon, I knew that I was madly in love with him. Finally, on Jan. 21st, 1973, David popped the question but without the ring. Of course, I said "yes" and felt certain he was saving the ring until Valentine's Day. Imagine my disappointment when that romantic day came and went without any fanfare (or ring). The next day however, he invited me to an expensive steak house in town and asked me to wear the dress I'd worn for our first date. I'd lent it to a friend and had to ask for it back. We enjoyed a wonderful meal. We talked about all the funny things that happened and how popular The Joyful Sound was.

"We've had it great so far haven't we?" I agreed and then he said, "Will you marry me?"

"Yes, of course," I said, a little puzzled because I'd already said yes back in January. He then reached into his pocket and pulled out the most gorgeous ring I'd ever seen and placed it on my finger. Because it was an expensive restaurant, the lights were too dim for me to see it clearly. I wanted to get a good look at it, so David asked for the bill and we went out to the streetlights. He told me later the reason he didn't give me the ring on Valentine's Day, he wanted my ring to be special. He had driven to a jeweller's shop in Toronto and had personally chosen the setting and the diamonds himself, but it wasn't going to be ready to be picked up on February 14th.

After David had put the ring on my finger, I wanted to tell the world, so we drove to his mom and dad's house; then to my place to show my family. They were all thrilled. I was in heaven. The next day at work I showed off my ring and all were impressed. I floated throughout the day. The band members were happy for us, later, when we showed them. A couple of them asked David what took him so long. He got a lot of well-deserved chiding because he had dragged his heels.

"We knew you two would be perfect for each other as soon as you joined our group," they all said. They were right.

If you are married, what is your engagement story? Although David *did* drag his heels, I'm glad he was cautious. That was probably the reason no one had snatched him up before we met. Caution can be a good thing, especially for such an important decision as marriage. After all, 'til death do us part can be an awfully long time.

I chased David until he caught me!

Another Engagement

> *... For wherever you go, I will go; And wherever you lodge, I will lodge; Your people shall be my people, And Your God, my God.*
> **Ruth 1:16b**

About a year after I'd moved out on my own, Mom and Jane decided to move back to Waterloo from Sarnia. Mom purchased a small three-unit apartment building near the church with the money from the sale of her home to Hank and Janet. Mom had no desire to date or remarry as she was quite content with her life. However, Ken was a long-time member of our church and took a shine toward Mom. He liked what he saw and asked our minister what he thought his chances would be. Pastor Shrier just laughed and said, "You won't have a chance with Florence Dubrick." But Ken proved him wrong. Soon Mom realized she too had an attraction to Ken, and they began dating. I must admit how weird it felt to have my mother dating and becoming engaged around the same time as David and I did, but we felt certain Ken would make her happy.

Just before they met, Mom needed a newer car as her old one had been giving her trouble, so she prayed about it. Mom would always laugh later when she would say, "I prayed for a car and God not only gave me a new car, but a chauffeur too!"

David and I were married in August 1973, and Mom and Ken were married in September of the same year. Mom sold the apartment building and moved into Ken's home nearby. They acted like kids and were deliriously happy. They travelled to Florida most winters and took their bicycles to places like Niagara Falls, where they stayed in motels so they could bike on the many beautiful, paved paths. Life continued to be good for them and God blessed their marriage.

Sometimes God doesn't answer our prayers as we planned, but as in the case with Mom, He did even better than what she'd ever dreamed. Her prayer for a car was answered in a way that far exceeded anything she could have imagined. Remember that God knows the future and He knows exactly what we need – even if we don't!

Mom and Ken had a happy life together.

Wedding Preparations

> *For I know the thoughts that I think toward you, says the LORD, thoughts of peace and not of evil, to give you a future and a hope.*
> **Jeremiah 29:11**

As soon as we knew we would be getting married, David and I talked about a date for the ceremony. David cautiously said, "Well Nancy, deCycles is coming through Waterloo (where our church was) on August 4th. Would you like to have them as part of our wedding?" This thought intrigued me, and we phoned the director, Bob Hardley, in Indiana and asked him if he'd be interested. He loved the idea and immediately said "Yes!"

The deCycles group is a high adventure Christian organization and that year they would be bicycling 3300 miles from Hartford City, Indiana, through Quebec, into Ontario, and back down to Indiana in four weeks. There were 54 young male riders, including David. Because they still would have five days to go after our wedding in Waterloo, I would either have to wait for my husband, or spend the first week of my honeymoon with them. I wasn't going to be without my new husband, so they arranged it that I could go along in our car while David stayed with the group all day. The 54 young men were all on bicycles and David would patrol back and forth on his motorcycle to help change tires, look for lost groups, and assist anyone in trouble. I still have the honoured distinction to be the first woman ever allowed on a deCycles trip, even though I was going to be in a car. (In 1975 it changed to co-ed, but my title still holds.)

My mother pretty much told me that she would make her own dress and be happy to attend my wedding, but that would be about the extent. I didn't care one bit, for this would be our wedding and we were paying for it.

I remember one Sunday afternoon in February when we were visiting my brother-in-law Hank's parents' place for lunch. Our wedding date, August 4th, seemed *so* far away and I lamented that it would never come. Mrs. Sonnenberg with her German accent assured me, "It will be here before you know it. She was right. In fact, as of this writing, August 4th has come and gone over 47 times.

For a few months before the wedding, I suffered from frequent gallbladder attacks. I did not want to suffer an attack on my wedding day or honeymoon, so I asked the doctor if I could have the gall bladder surgery he had suggested before my wedding. He agreed and booked it for June 12th, my 23rd birthday. Happy Birthday Nancy!

These days it is a simple procedure but back in 1973 it was major surgery, and it took some time to recover. I didn't mind though, because it gave me even more time to plan, plan, plan; more time to get ready for the big day.

Have you ever noticed how some days drag by so slowly that you must check the clock to see if it's ticking? Yet other days fly by so fast it leaves you breathless? How thankful I am that each one of us has the same number of hours every day. How we spend that time is up to us. I for one, want my days to count. That also means we need to rest when our body says rest and to do and look for opportunities to help and encourage others. Each day is precious.

The founders of deCycles, Bob and Dory Hardley, and us.

August 4th, 1973 – The Big Day

He who finds a wife finds a good thing, And obtains favor from the LORD. **Proverbs 18:22**

A not-so-good part of our spectacular deCycles wedding was that David had to leave me three weeks before our big day in order to join the bicycle tour. Having so much time to myself made me lonely. However, being the consummate planner, I tried to keep busy by finalizing even the smallest details to make our wedding day perfect.

David did surprise me a couple of days before the wedding by standing at the doorway of my office building waiting for me to come out. He'd left deCycles in Niagara Falls, Canada just to be with me. He surprised me so perfectly that I screamed and ran into his arms nearly knocking him over!

I requested at work to have the Friday off before our wedding, so I drove to where I knew the deCycles would be stopping for lunch on their way into Waterloo and met David and the 54 young men. What a great time I had and thoroughly enjoyed all the attention.

The wedding rehearsal went well that evening, and I was so excited I didn't think I would sleep. But I must have because I woke up refreshed.

"Today is my wedding day!"

I jumped out of bed to look outside and saw fluffy white clouds perfectly pictured against a beautiful blue sky and knew it would be a perfect day.

Finally, standing at the back of the church, I could hardly wait to face my groom. I determined that I would not look anywhere but into David's handsome face all the way down the aisle and I kept that promise. No one else mattered in that full church but my beloved soon-to-be husband. Pastor Shrier and my Uncle Ralph both helped lead the service and I eagerly looked forward to hearing those precious words.

"I now pronounce you husband and wife. You may kiss the bride."

But it never happened!

All too soon we were walking toward the unity candle. Our mothers had already lit the two separate candles at the beginning of the ceremony. Now it was our turn to light the middle one and blow out our individual candles, symbolizing that we had become one. My veil still covered my face, because David hadn't been given permission to lift it up to give me my kiss. That meant I had to pull my own veil away (without setting it on fire) to blow out the candle. We still laugh about it. My cousin John told us years later that his father (my Uncle Ralph) saw such love in our eyes for each other that he lost his place during the ceremony. Our joke for years is that we were "living in sin" because we never were formally pronounced man and wife. However, we have the marriage certificate to prove that we are indeed married. Sweet relief!

When we went outside the church, the 54 young men from deCycles had created an honour guard tunnel for us with their bicycle flags. As we walked through, they lowered the flags. A local T.V. station filmed this part of our unique ceremony and aired it the next day. Of course, back then no one had a way to record the moment so we just have the memory. But those who did see it on television said it was wonderful to watch.

Our local newspaper came, too, and we have a huge picture of David and me with the honour guard. What a truly awesome sight.

Just as many other little girls, I always dreamed of my wedding, but never could I have imagined the fantastic day I ended up having. Such a spectacular event that many people still comment on it.

Do you have any beautiful memories of an important occasion? If so, relive them when things are not going so well. There is something therapeutic when we think of the happy times in the past and this can give us the energy and the lift to continue life in the present.

August 4, 1973. I thought this day would never come! Left to Right: Jane Dubrick, Janet Bredin, Janet Sonnenberg, Me, David, Terry Seiling, Ronald Seiling, Jeffrey Seiling.

Honeymoon

A man's heart plans his way, But the LORD directs his steps.
Proverbs 16:9

David and I spent two romantic nights together before he had to report for duty with the cycling crew. When we finally got to the church Monday morning, deCycles were long gone. Attached to David's motorcycle was a note letting him know the road they would be taking. He jumped on his motorcycle and I followed behind in our little Toyota. Our unique adventure as newlyweds had begun.

We finally caught up to the group just before the U.S. border. When we crossed into Michigan, the town had a police escort ready for the group. David took his position at the front beside the police and I was told to stay at the rear. Because the police escorted the group, they were led through all the red lights and stop signs. Because I was not a rule-breaker, I stopped at each one. The bicycles with their red flags waving grew farther and farther ahead of me. I began to panic. To my horror, in the distance I could see a drawbridge being raised. The closer I got to the bridge, the more my heart sank. Everyone else had made it over but me. I almost stood up behind the wheel and shouted, "Noooooo!" It seemed like an eternity before that bridge went down and when I got to the other side there were no bicycles in sight. I've never been good with directions, (inherited from my parents) but I didn't think I needed to care because the plan was for me to stay with the group, bringing up the rear. With a sinking heart, I realized I was all alone. I drove around for a while, then turned onto a road.

"Have you seen any bicycles go past here?" I asked a man at a gas station. His blank stare said it all. He shook his head, probably wondering why he should notice a few bicycles.

My heart sank. My anxiety grew. I turned around and went in the other direction. I drove until I saw two old men sitting on their porch. I got out of the car and asked the same question. To my utter relief, the one pointed and said, "Yea! A hundred of 'em went that-a-way!" I didn't want to admit that I, a brand-new bride, had lost my husband amid that group of cyclists. I thanked the men and carried on. Soon, I saw the headlight of a motorcycle coming toward me. "Oh, dear God, let it be David." Much to my relief David, my knight-in-shining-armour, appeared. When he saw the familiar white Toyota, he did a U turn and I pulled over. I got out and hugged him tight, but I could see that he wasn't exactly pleased with me. His first words were, "What happened to you?" With tears I explained. "Each red light and stop sign that you went through, the farther behind I got and then the bridge came up and I had no idea what road to go down." He hugged me, chuckled and said, "Honey, when you're in a police escort, you can go through the lights too!"

"Well, nobody told me!"

Apparently, the police accompanied the bicycles a few miles out of town, and David didn't notice I wasn't with them until all the riders were in their groups. He wondered how he would explain about losing his new bride in another country two days after the wedding. It was more frightening for me at the time, than funny, but now when we look back, we have a good giggle.

The deCycles Honour Guard. The KW Record and CKCO TV were on hand to record the "Wedding of the Century." Police escort and everything!

The "Lost Bride" story has been repeated so many times that we've lost count. Although it portrayed a panic situation at the time, it turned out to be a story that guarantees laughter and makes everyone happy. Once again, it shows us that God truly can turn a difficult situation into something of rare beauty.

1973. The 54 young men with whom I spent the first week of my honeymoon.

Back to Reality

Finally, my brethren, be strong in the Lord and in the power of His might. **Ephesians 6: 10**

The young men treated me like a Queen on the deCycles trip and it turned out to be a most glorious honeymoon. We talked about putting a "Just Married" sign on our little white Toyota and a sign on David's motorcycle that said, "Me too!" Not too many brides are alone in the car all day while her husband is busy patrolling 54 young men on bicycles, but the overall "uniqueness" was well worth the sacrifice.

The days were long, but we eagerly looked forward to spending each night together. After the deCycles trip finished, David and I continued on to the Smoky Mountains to enjoy the rest of our honeymoon. Reluctantly, when the time came, we returned home to our little apartment and fulltime jobs.

The next summer, David went on another deCycles trip, but I couldn't go. I felt miserable. I'd never been alone before since we were married.

To make matters worse, I received the awful news that David had been in a serious motorcycle accident. Ironically, he had been on his way to get help for a rider who had crashed and needed medical help. David spent a few days in the hospital far away and I couldn't get to him. Not only was I working full time, but the group was in the midwestern United States. David kept reassuring me over the phone that there was nothing I could do, and to save my vacation time for when we could be together. Thankfully, he did recover. God had sent His angels to protect him from certain death. What a glorious reunion David and I had when the trip was over.

The next year, deCycles went co-ed and I joined the staff. I asked for an extra week off work, and my boss graciously gave it to me. David's employer seemed accustomed to David taking extra time off from work, so it worked well for us both.

That time, I was in a support vehicle all by myself and had to really stretch to be able to push the gas pedal (short legs.) I moved the seat as close as it could go, but my foot cramped constantly. Even though the pain made me grimace, how could I possibly complain about a sore foot when the riders were bravely pedaling 80 to 100 miles each day no matter what the weather? My most despised job occurred daily when I would have to go to the town where we would be spending the night and knocking on church doors, asking if we could stay there. Back then, that wasn't uncommon. I'd scan the horizon looking for church steeples and head toward them. I'd quake every time I'd have to walk up to a church. Some ministers or priests were welcoming, and other times I came away empty. For someone who can't stand rejection, there couldn't have been a worse job for me. I did find a place each night for the riders to sleep, but it certainly placed me greatly out of my comfort zone.

Lots of good life lessons came out of those trips with the deCycles, and many lives have been impacted because of this unique ministry. It is still going today and our two boys, family, friends, and even our granddaughter, Samara, have experienced this one-of-a-kind experience. We volunteered on many trips since then as staff and always came away exhausted but feeling accomplished.

It is true that we grow through trials. I heard somewhere that both coal and diamonds, are made from the same substance. It's the pressure put on each that makes the difference.

True. It is never easy or comfortable to go through hard times but, oh, the rewards if we come out on the other side with greater wisdom and experience. We should never waste our trials.

Minister of Youth

But He said, "The things which are impossible with men are possible with God." **Luke 18:27**

David and I loved married life. We enjoyed the thrill of living together and learning each other's preferences and habits. Early on, however, we realized we each had to have our own tube of toothpaste. David's way was to carefully roll the tube up. I would gleefully squeeze it in the middle. Frustrated, David bought me my own tube to use as I pleased. We still chuckle over our differences in that department.

I worked at the University of Waterloo and David secured a position at Home Hardware. We were still singing with The Joyful Sound and David joined my children's ministry. We became a dynamic team.

A year after we were married, our Pastor asked David to take on the duties as Minister of Youth at our church. Pastor Shrier knew David didn't have any formal Bible School training, but he saw his strong Christian upbringing as an asset to the youth at WPA. David said yes and quit his job to join the ministry team.

At that time, our Youth department at the church rivaled the size of some larger congregations, so the responsibility would keep him busy. Most holiday Mondays were spent with the youth, and of course I went along. Sometimes though, I resented the time we had to spend with the youth because I had to work, too. But I have since repented of my selfishness!

One time, David organized a "Wake-a-thon," a fundraiser for youth retreats. It began Friday evening and ended Sunday afternoon, which meant that he had to plan a lot of activities to keep the kids awake. Our church had a Sunday School bus that needed painting, so with paintbrushes and paint rollers and blue paint they did a good job transforming the ugly yellow bus into a thing of beauty.

Another time, David planned a '60s night where everyone came dressed in the fashion of that era. We all had a blast in the school gym across the street from the church.

There were highs and lows in David's new position, but we did our best and trusted that lives were touched through our efforts.

We were still involved in deCycles every summer. One year, Paul Shrier (Pastor Shrier's oldest son) joined and eventually earned "The Most Improved Rider" award. The training, although tough for the first couple of weeks, helped Paul gain more strength and stamina and he made us all proud with his efforts. Years later he went on to get his PhD in California and admitted that deCycles was one of the reasons he could take on such a huge undertaking. He often said, "If I can travel 4,300 miles in five and a half weeks on a heavy 10-speed bicycle, I can do anything." Indeed, this amazing ministry has had, and continues to have, a great impact on all who choose this unique adventure.

How young we were!

Do you have an experience that changed your life for the better? It doesn't have to be as dramatic as pedaling 4,300 miles on a bicycle, but whatever the moment, dig deep and remember it from time to time and be thankful for that memory.

Funny deCycles' Stories

The fear of the LORD is the instruction of wisdom, And before honor is humility. **Proverbs 15:33**

I don't think I'm alone in my confusion. (Well maybe this is where you can at least humour me a little.) Have you ever had a kind of mental block as you try to pronounce certain words? Take the nearby city of Guelph, Ontario for instance. Unless you are from this area, it might be difficult to decipher. It is pronounced, "Gwelf." (you're welcome.)

On one deCycles trip where we volunteered, David drove the big truck that held all the sleeping bags, duffle bags, and bicycle parts. I was along for the ride and liked to think of myself as good company for David. We would stick with the group of 60 riders all day until mid-afternoon. Then we'd proceed to the pre-arranged church where we were to stay overnight to let them know the cyclists were on the way. No more knocking on church doors!

That particular day we were to stay in Savannah, Georgia. We'd just passed a mileage sign and I said to David, "Oh Look. We've only 15 miles to ..." and then I pronounced it, "Sa-vi-nah." David looked over at me puzzled and said, "Where did you say?" Now I became puzzled, because we all knew we were going to Savannah, so I said it again. He asked me to repeat it a few times, but each time I pronounced it the same way. To be perfectly clear, I was getting tired of it. Finally, he laughed and said, "Nancy, it's pronounced Suh-van-na – like Vanna White." Oh, my brain. How I howled!

We arrived and discussed particulars with the office secretary, checking the place out until the bicycle riders started to arrive. I welcomed the first group with, "Welcome to Sa-vi-nah!" I'd said it again. They laughed and I must admit my embarrassment shone through in the form of a rather red face. The problem continued because it wasn't the only time I did it and I truly felt humiliated. I kept my mouth shut after that!

While we were there, some parishioners came to see our group (they often came to witness for themselves this unique event.) They handed out leftover green t-shirts that announced a Rock-and-Roll

Festival they'd had a couple of years ago. David treasures that shirt because he is a real fan of 1950s and 60s music.

Decades later, while reading in the living room, David pointed to his Savannah shirt and said, "What city is this?" Now I honestly thought before I spoke, and slowly said, "Sa-vi-nah." I waited for his "hurray!" but it didn't come. It then dawned on me that I'd done it again and howled once more.

At least only David witnessed it this time, and we did have a good laugh.

"Suh-van-na, Suh-van-na, Suh-van-na!" I think I finally have it – I think.

Do you have a funny story about mispronouncing words? Don't feel as if you are alone, and certainly don't feel embarrassed about it (like I did at the time.) Instead, shout it to the world and that will not only make others have a good laugh, but it will take the sting out of your gaffe. Everyone will feel better for it.

I always wanted to say that I went to Harvard.

The largest deCycles group ever – 2014.

And Then There Were Three

Behold, children are a heritage from the LORD, The fruit of the womb is a reward. **Psalm 127:3**

We decided to start a family 15 months after we were married but I was having difficulty getting pregnant. I'll never forget when my doctor finally gave me the news over the phone that the last pregnancy test came back positive. My screams must have hurt the poor guy's eardrums. David could barely contain his joy, too. From the moment I knew I was carrying a baby under my heart, I prayed for him or her every day. I knew this child was a gift from God and I wanted us to be the best parents possible to our blessing-to-come.

August 25, 1976 brought us a beautiful baby boy we named Nathan David. To our heartache, he was born with severe bilateral club foot and required plaster casts when only two days old. David brought some magic markers into the hospital and painted a Canadian flag on the toes of the tiny casts, and a lightning bolt with "Captain Canada" written sideways. Nathan soon became the darling of the nursery.

I remember shedding many tears when I realized that our precious baby boy had club foot because of something in my genetic makeup. David held me when I told him how sorry I was that he married someone who unknowingly carried the gene. I lamented that if he had married someone else, he would have a boy who could enjoy sports as much as he did. David would not let me talk this way, but that guilt (unfounded as it was) would stay with me for decades.

Hospitals, at the time, kept new mothers in for a week, but on the sixth day I began to hemorrhage severely. The head nurse contacted the doctor right away. She received her orders and yelled at the other nurses to get the blood hung and ready to go once they received it. They even put a cuff on the bag to force it into my veins faster. Because the blood was cold, I began to shake uncontrollably. The doctor assessed me and decided there were few options. They rushed me into surgery and were able to stop the hemorrhage. Had I not still been in the hospital, I would have died. We lived more than 45 minutes away and would never have made it to the hospital in time. God, once again, spared my life.

Nathan thrived well despite his club feet. Nothing could keep him down. He learned how to crawl with casts (wearing the knees out of his little pants) and then he was fitted with special shoes and a bar that kept his feet apart. One time he somehow got his legs under the couch and called me to come. When I saw him, he disgustedly said, "Guck Mommy, Guck." He meant "stuck", but his cuteness made me smile. He had a little waddle that entertained many showing his dogged determination to get around. This determination has served him well all his life. Nathan has overcome many challenges with the same attitude he had when he was a baby.

Nathan born August 25th, 1976.

Trust God entirely, even when you do not understand what He is doing. The important thing to remember is that God is not in Heaven wringing His hands, wondering what to do with your situation. He has a plan.

Life Can Be A Challenge

> *Now may the God of hope fill you with all joy and peace in believing, that you may abound in hope by the power of the Holy Spirit.* **Romans 15:13**

Poor Nathan wore many casts, bars, and endured three surgeries to correct his club feet. The final surgery took place just before his third birthday. I was pregnant with our second child and was waiting in his hospital room for him to come out of recovery. When they wheeled his little crib in, I leaned over him and told him how much I loved him. He looked up at me with a sad little face and shook his head slowly and whimpered, "N-o-o-o. N-o-o-o." My heart almost broke and with tears said, "Oh Honey, if we didn't allow the doctors to operate, you wouldn't be able to walk, or run, or play sports like your daddy." Of course, his little mind could not possibly comprehend my words.

We had no idea how much pain our little boy endured, for he never complained. In fact, he played hockey in the winter and baseball in the summer and excelled. Nathan was always the shortest kid because his legs never grew properly but was usually one of the strongest. At one out-of-town baseball game, my buttons almost popped off when his coach came up to me after the game and said, "I wish I had a whole team like your son Nathan. He is a determined little guy."

Fact is, he lived in such great pain that when he became an adult, he opted for a second opinion. The doctor ordered x-rays right away. Nathan never had x-rays on his feet before. So, when the doctor showed Nathan his x-rays and asked, "When did you break your foot?" he was taken aback.

"I didn't break my foot," Nathan replied.

"Well, you most certainly did. It's right here!" the doctor pointed to the x-ray image. Go ask your parents, they'll know." Nathan remembered jumping out of a tree on the farm and his foot hurting a bit more than usual, but he continued to walk on it because "it only hurt a bit more."

Proud Parents. Nathan with casts.

To this day he has multiple problems that stem from his feet, but he rarely complains. His motto is that his club foot problems made him the man he is today. We all greatly admire his amazing attitude.

Over the years, I have spoken at many women's events and usually comment on the story of Nathan's reaction as a three-year-old to his surgery. I would explain that there are times when God allows something into our lives, and we look up from our "cribs" and say "N-o-o-o. N-o-o-o." God wants to tell us why it is important that we face trials. But He also knows our minds cannot always comprehend why. God's ways are always best, and He knows exactly what we need for the future. Trust Him. Father does know best.

Our Family Grows

Behold, how good and how pleasant it is For brethren to dwell together unity! **Psalm 133:1**

I had always felt sorry for my childhood friend, Valerie, because she had no brothers or sisters. I remembered that, so I knew I didn't want Nathan to grow up as an only child. When he turned two, we decided the time had come to have another child. On May 3, 1979, we welcomed another son we named Matthew Robert into the family. Nathan loved him right away and became the best big brother ever.

Soon I had my hands full as a busy mother of two, and David had a fulltime job selling and servicing milking equipment. One day, when the phone rang while we were eating, David spoke to a farmer who was having some difficulty with his milkers. After hearing the conversation, the boys knew their daddy would have to leave again. He had no choice because of the demands of his job, but it was difficult for all of us. This happened many times and it never got any easier.

I remember one early evening, sitting on the front porch feeling sorry for myself because David had to go out on yet another call. Suddenly two motorcycles roared in our long laneway. I brightened to see four of my relatives having the time of their lives. I guess I did not look my usual joyful self. Because I am usually a cheerful person, they immediately saw that something wasn't right.

"What's wrong Nancy?" one of them asked.

"David's on another call, and I'm left alone here with the boys again."

Instead of cheering me up, they just laughed and said, "Well, every dog has their day. We've had ours and now it's your turn."

With that, they turned around and roared out of our lane. So much for a bit of compassion. Needless to say, I felt worse than ever. Many years later I shared with them how it had hurt me, but they still thought it was simply hilarious. I must admit this was one time I didn't laugh.

I found it extremely difficult to let Nathan go for his first day of school. I remember walking him to the end of our lane early that first morning and crying all the way back to the house. When David saw me, he said, "It's not like you sent him off to war you know!" I had to smile but clung to Matthew all the harder.

Matthew was born with a smile on his face on May 3rd, 1979.

Then the day came when I walked both Nathan and Matthew down our lane but this time the house was empty when I returned. That was hard. However, the boys loved school and did very well. I became involved in all the activities and school trips and became almost as much a part of the staff as the teachers. It pleased me to be voted the president of the PTA and I enjoyed helping to plan fundraisers for new playground equipment which turned out to be a huge success.

By this time, both boys had been practicing and each became ventriloquists. Like parents, like children. Nathan had a Mickey Mouse ventriloquist doll he called "Charlie Church Mouse" and Matthew had a monkey puppet he named Eeek-Eeek the Monkey. The Seiling Family emerged. I had many dreams as a little girl, including marrying a kind Christian man, having children, and living happily ever after. Of course, no one lives completely happily ever after, but God did grant me the desires of my heart. I felt fulfilled as a wife and mother.

What were your dreams? Were they fulfilled? If not, did it bother you? Did it change the direction of your life? Sometimes we live in a pie-in-the-sky dream world that simply is not practical. Reality may step in, but that doesn't mean your life won't have meaning. Trust the One who knows the path you should take.

Matthew

But if anyone loves God, this one is known by Him.
1 Corinthians 8:3

It is always interesting how children who are raised by the same parents can be so different. Nathan was quiet, intelligent, and inquisitive when it came to learning new things. Matthew was smart, energetic, and loved animals. He would have lived in the barn had we allowed him. His love for animals carried on into his adult life and he fulfilled his dream of owning a petting farm.

One day while visiting Matt's wife—Sarah, and my two grandchildren, Sarah brought out an old school binder that I'd made for each of our boys. This binder, separated into grades complete with pictures and report cards and anything else that I figured would be special in the years to come, sparked sweet memories. Matt's binder was chock full and falling apart, but oh, the precious memories inside. His grade 2 teacher had them write in journals and Matt's entries were priceless. He loved to talk about all his friends (and he had many) and what they did at recess. I think recess ranked as his favourite subject! Oh, how I loved the journal. Here are a few excerpts complete with original spelling:

> **March 8, 1987**
> I brot my crasy carpit to school and am smashing all the people on my crasy carpit. It is fun!

I discovered why the teachers would tell me that Matt needed to be more respectful to others at recess!

> **March 12, 1987**
> I have had a stumic ache for 4 weeks. Dr. Bender nose why I have been sick. It's my stumic. I am taking powders.

Oh my, how I howled. Nothing got past Dr. Bender. We paid him the big bucks to have him tell us Matthew's problem with stomach aches is his "stumic." (The remedies he gave to Matthew did help, so we thank you Dr. Bender.)

December 8, 1987
It will be Christmas soon and I think my big gift is Lego and I like my mom. My mom is nice and my dad is nice too. I like my mom and dad. They are nice.
The teacher added, "I think they are pretty nice too."

January 8, 1988
I got a bike and some Lego. It is asom and some candy. I like Christmas. I like my mom and dad.

In the spring of 1988, he wrote:

My mom is coming with us to a maple sugar bush. I like my mom. Everyone likes my mom.

My heart melted. We all do the best while raising our children and to read these precious words meant more than any gift.

There's nothing quite like the honesty and the innocence of children. I love how the teachers made them keep journals. They seem to be more meaningful as the years go along. Take time to talk to a child. We all need their wisdom and delightful insights.

Family picture around this time.

Performing as the Seiling Family

Finally, all of you be of one mind, having compassion for one another; love as brothers, be tenderhearted, be courteous;
1 Peter 3:8

Life continued to be happy and fulfilling, with a few trials mixed in to keep us on our toes and growing in our faith. Most weekends found us travelling to a different city to put on programs. The audiences seemed to enjoy our shows and thought Nathan and Matthew were adorable. They learned quickly how to behave both on and off stage and interact with complete strangers. This gave them self-assurance without being arrogant and it has greatly helped them through life in their professions.

We often laugh at how one weekend we had an engagement on a Saturday evening and one again in the opposite direction on Sunday morning. The boys had fallen asleep on the way home. Luckily, I had anticipated this so, earlier they had changed into their pajamas. When we got home, David carried them, still sleeping, to their own beds. Early the next morning, he carried them back out to the car. They awoke when we were well on our way and I had a light breakfast ready. I then changed them into their Sunday clothes as soon as we got to the church. As far as Nathan and Matthew were concerned, they slept in the car all night! They liked that.

Such is the life of performers. It often looks glamorous to be on stage, but few people understand how difficult it can be behind the scenes. However, it is well worth it knowing we were giving a good program with lots of laughter and the message of God's love.

It is so easy to envy entertainers, but difficult to understand what it takes to learn the craft and what a challenge it could be to get to each venue on time no matter what the weather or how we felt. Next time you go to a show or program, make sure and say thank you. It will mean a lot to them.

100 Huntley Street

Preach the word! Be ready in season and out of season.
2 Timothy 4:2a

Much to our delight, in 1984, we were invited to be on-air guests for a live Christian TV show, *100 Huntley Street*. Each summer the staff there produced *The Club House* for children in the live studio audience and they wanted us to do one segment each day for five days. They requested that we each bring along five different outfits, so I had a lot of packing to do. We stayed in a lovely hotel and got to go swimming every day and eat out every evening. One of the staff joined us for breakfast and took us to the studio in the morning and back to the hotel every afternoon. We felt like celebrities and were treated well.

My responsibility to come up with five different skits for our puppets proved to be quite a challenge. The second year we were asked again, and that made the challenge even harder, but it worked, and we were well received.

Neither my Uncle Len nor I could have ever imagined how far-reaching Jerry would become, nor that my husband and children would each have their own ventriloquist dolls and become an integral part of our ministry, too. God had a plan for my life, and He has a plan for yours also. He may not ask you to be a ventriloquist or a singer, but the important thing is to be willing to listen and to obey. It may surprise you what He has in store. Just don't ask to be a ventriloquist. We already have enough of them around here.

Thrill of a Lifetime

Do not be deceived, God is not mocked; For whatever a man sows, that will he also reap. **Galatians 6:7**

Another one of the highlights in our life happened when we were chosen to be guests on a Canadian television program, *Thrill of a Lifetime*. This weekly show focussed on people who had written to them, describing what their "thrill" might look like. One husband and wife wanted to build an igloo and sleep in it, so the producers flew them to the Arctic where they were shown how to build an igloo while the camera crew filmed them in action. Then the couple spent the night in it, fulfilling their dream. Another person wanted to ski behind a ferry boat. A couple wrote in to say they wanted to eat breakfast in Newfoundland, lunch in Toronto at the CN Tower, and dinner in Vancouver. Again, the producers made it happen.

My thrill of a lifetime was to meet a ventriloquist who I had admired for years—Shari Lewis and Lambchop. I remember buying a stamp at the post office and shielding the address from the clerk because I felt a little embarrassed sending off my request to meet Shari and Lambchop. I thought the postal clerk might have wondered who I thought I was to be asking for a favour from this popular television show. However, my embarrassment turned to joy when a producer called and said they were interested.

"Are you any good?" the person on the other end of the phone asked.

How does one answer that without bragging? They must have been impressed with the telephone interview but said they needed us to come to the studio in Toronto on a certain date to meet us in person. They wanted to make sure we actually were good enough to meet Shari Lewis.

When we arrived at the studio, we were driven to a pancake restaurant and seated at a round table. The announcer said, "Here are the Seilings eating a normal breakfast. However, …" Then they stopped the camera, had us sit very still and handed Jerry, Norton, and Charlie Church Mouse to us. The camera rolled again and

BLING! There we were, holding our puppets. The voice-over continued; "The Seilings are not your ordinary family."

After the producers were satisfied with what was filmed, someone from the crew drove us to a school and told us to entertain the kids. The children liked the skit and then we sang a song with Jerry and Norton—again and again. It became very tiring because they kept moving the camera to get different angles and I just about collapsed when they said, "One more time." I almost refused but decided to do it one more time. Just as we were singing the song, we heard someone singing along with us. Great, I thought. The kids have heard it so often, they know it by heart and the director is going to say, "Cut!" and we'll have to do it yet again.

Imagine our surprise when we spotted Shari Lewis and Lambchop coming in our direction and singing along with us. I didn't realize it at the time, but I tapped Jerry on the shoulder and said, "Jerry, that's Shari Lewis!" Nathan said that at the time he wondered why I told Jerry instead of him. After all, he was a real person and Jerry wasn't! Shari really took a shine to Nathan and Charlie Church Mouse and the results were precious. She was a consummate professional, and we were in awe that she seemed to enjoy spending time with us as much as we did with her. Far too soon it was over. She was whisked away for another personal experience.

The crew zipped us back to a gorgeous hotel with two rooms — one for us and an adjoining one for the boys, plus they gave us a hefty food allowance. The organization certainly lived up to their name, "Thrill of a Lifetime!"

What "Thrill of a Lifetime" would you choose if you could? Sometimes all we need to do is ask God. Never in my wildest dreams did I imagine meeting the famous Shari Lewis yet meet her we did. God loves to give gifts to His children, just as we love to shower our children with things that make them happy.

This is the promo photo we used for Thrill of a Lifetime. 1984

Seiling Family Ministries

But we have this treasure in earthen vessels, that the excellence of the power may be of God and not of us. **2 Corinthians 4:7**

Our family kept busy. Being invited to many church camps for five or six days at a time kept us hopping. At the camps, the adults had their own services and the children had theirs. I'd have to work long hours to get enough material to fill in the time for these sessions. David and the boys would plan sports activities so I could have a break in-between. Of course, Jerry, Norton, Charlie, and Eeek-Eeek were always there, plus I created object lessons, Bible lessons, crafts, and a final story each day. It wore me out, most days, by the time we sent the kids to their parents, but it felt good to accomplish so much.

One of the activities the children loved centred around memorizing Scripture verses. When the children had memorized all five scriptures in their booklets, they were told to ask as many adults as they could find during the day to listen to them recite these Bible verses. Then they would ask the adult to sign their booklet. The ones with the most signatures won prizes at the end of the week. It worked well and the adults were deeply impressed at how many children knew the verses. They were more than willing to hear their recitations and to sign their names.

Each day I shared a story that would always end with a cliffhanger. When I'd say, "And you have to come back tomorrow to find out what happened," the kids would groan. Wait a whole day to find out the identity of the scary stranger, or, what happened to Danny? Did he fall all the way to the bottom of the ravine? Would Annette freeze to death with her sprained ankle in the snow because she said she's going to bed but instead went for a walk in the moonlight? I must say that their reactions always amused me, and I knew that for sure they'd come back to hear how the story turned out!

One cute story occurred when we were the entertainment at a small-town fair. There were some girls there who were part of the "Queen of the Fair and Her Court" and they were going to be

The photographer got a kick out of our family. 1993.

appearing on stage. We were in a room with them before the program began and Nathan (around 10 years old at the time) asked, "Why are they so nervous?" We explained that they would be going on stage and it frightened them. We could see the wheels turning in his mind and the explanation that they were nervous simply because they would be on stage didn't compute. Fact is, we took Nathan and Matthew from infants to as many of our performances as we could, and they often assisted us. To be on stage equalled fun—no big deal to them! Our boys have often thanked us for the many opportunities they had because of our programs. Few of their friends had the adventures they did, and they have many fond memories of our times together.

Do you remember hearing stories read to you that intrigued you or did you read a book that you especially enjoyed? Perhaps you should take it off the shelf and re-read it. There are so many excellent books for children that are classics, and you may surprise yourself by how much you remember.

Dream Home

> *Unless the LORD builds the house, They labor in vain who build it; Unless the LORD guards the city, The watchman stays awake in vain.* **Psalm 127:1**

During this period, we sold our small farm and were able to sever almost two acres of property across the wooded creek. In fact, let me share a humorous story about the severance.

It is quite difficult to sever a property, but we felt the time had come to leave the farm and build our dream home—a Cape Cod-style home with a full wrap-around porch and three dormers. We inquired as to what we needed to do and filled in all the required paperwork. The day came to meet with the severance committee and to hear them say yea or nay. This committee held our future in their hands, but, although we were nervous, we had prayed often about it. So, we stood tall and walked into the building hand in hand. When we arrived, we saw other people in the waiting room also seeking severances. We were shocked that they all had lawyers with them. Lawyers? Oh no. We should have hired a lawyer! Too late. Our names were called, and we walked into the board room. Seven men and women looking serious, looked back at us. However, before we sat down, I noticed Mr. Green. I couldn't help smiling.

"Mr. Green. You may not remember us, but you were Nathan and Matthew Seiling's bus driver." He looked at us knowingly.

"You used to give each child on your route one of those thick chocolate bars every Christmas and our boys thought they'd hit the jackpot!" Mr. Green laughed.

"Of course, I remember your boys. I remember when Nathan attended kindergarten, he was so small that I'd have to help him up the steps of the bus." The atmosphere seemed less tense as Mr. Green continued.

"Then, because Nathan was the last one to be dropped off, the poor little tyke would fall asleep and I'd have to go back and wake him up at your stop."

Everyone in the room laughed and I wondered a little what the people in the waiting room were thinking. Mr. Green then softly added, "And I remember that you used to write me the loveliest thank-you notes, Christmas cards, and oh those homemade goodies you sent along. That touched me deeply." Soon our petition for severance came to a vote and it passed in our favour. Without a doubt, God had Mr. Green on that committee, and it swayed the vote in our favour, even without a lawyer. We thanked them very much and walked sedately to the elevator. Once the elevator doors closed, we were in each other's arms saying, "We are going to have our dream home!" I jumped up and down, squealed with delight and we hugged some more, thanking God for His goodness.

Is there a time when you knew that God arranged for the right people to be at the right place, at the right time? Some say this is just a coincidence, but we know differently. I have to smile at this statement: "Coincidences stop happening when I stop praying." We did pray about it and left the decision in God's hands. He arranged who would be at that meeting long before we knew we would be there.

It took a lot of work, but it was well worth it.

Too Loud Nancy

These things I have spoken to you, that in Me you may have peace. In the world you will have tribulation; but be of good cheer, I have overcome the world." **John 16:33**

Right after we received the severance, our lives were a whirlwind for an entire year. We contracted some of the construction to professionals but decided to do much of the work ourselves. It turned out to be a grueling year and one I wouldn't want to repeat, but soon we had our beautiful home. We were absolutely thrilled and thankful for this incredible gift. But shortly after, I found myself in a dark place. It felt like a kind of personality crisis.

If anyone wanted to hurt me, they just needed to say, "Nancy, you are so loud!" I would crumble inside. It cut deeply and I would feel shattered. I never meant to be loud, so I'd cringe whenever someone uttered those five words. Suddenly, all the light and sunshine would slip away, and I'd slither into a corner and miserably wait until I could escape.

I decided I must be a despicable person and needed to change my personality. Over the years I would look at shy, quiet women and admire their poise—something I did not feel I had. This started me on a quest to transform myself into a woman no one would ever again accuse of being loud. I hated myself so much that whenever I passed by a mirror, I would actually stick my tongue out. I was in serious trouble.

Slowly but surely, I restrained myself from any outbursts of laughter or loud jesting. It was not easy to suppress my natural inclination to be joyful.

Sometimes someone would come up to me and say, "Nancy, are you alright?" I would politely and quietly answer.

"Yes, I'm just fine." Then I would smile and walk away with what I hoped came across as a stately, regal manner. That was who I thought I needed to be, after all.

Of course, I shared this with David, and he tried to reason with me, but I continued to be adamant that I had no choice but to change my personality.

It all came to a head when David and I were invited to our friend Lovada's home for a nice evening with our close friends. As we walked into the summer kitchen of her century old home, David said something that made me laugh. Lovada heard me and said, "I hear my Nancy!" Immediately I cringed inside and determined to stay with my "new Nancy" image the entire evening.

The party eventually split into two groups; At one point, I stood in the wide doorway that separated us. On my right were the intellectuals in the living room, who were debating about something out of my league, and on my left were the ones that were having a blast playing games, in the dining room. My head swiveled from side to side until I rested on the group enjoying a game with much laughter. That was where I belonged. I joined the laughing group and became Nancy again, much to David's relief.

One day, I met my friends for a luncheon. One of them said, "Oh good, there's loud Nancy!" Most of these gals knew exactly what that meant, and we had a good chuckle, but there was a couple who did not understand and wanted to hear my story. My story of how I became desperate to change my personality from outgoing, loud, and bubbly, to quiet and sophisticated. What a silly notion. God made me this way, and to try and change my personality was futile and just plain dumb! Now, when anyone calls me loud, I shrug and keep smiling.

Someone once said to me, "If we aren't who God made us to be, then the world is the loser." There's only one YOU, and your personality is unique. So instead of chiding yourself, realize that the world does need you. Rejoice and be free to be the one you were created to be. I lost a portion of my life trying to be something I wasn't. Take it from me, it simply won't work!

Lovada Kechnie, my dear friend since 1965.

In the Presence of a Star

Be glad in the LORD and rejoice, you righteous; And shout for joy, all you upright in heart! **Psalm 32:11**

One morning we took our van into the shop to have some minor noises checked before the warranty ran out. Dave, our mechanic, went with my David for a test drive, but, of course, the noises weren't there. Mechanic Dave had a great sense of humour. "Car parts talk to each other and they know when the mechanic is in the car."

"They're saying, 'Shhhhh.' Wait until he's gone before you make the noise again. This will make the new owners look stupid," added my David. The mechanic even pretended to get out of the van when they pulled to the side of the road and loudly said, "Well goodbye David, I'm going now," and then quietly climbed back in to "fool the van." Loved his sense of humor!

Then Dave the mechanic said, "I'll never forget when you and Nancy were hired to be the entertainment with your ventriloquist puppets for a banquet to honour Darryl Sittler. He was one of the best NHL hockey players with the Toronto Maple Leafs for years. Darryl's hometown, St. Jacobs, welcomed the hockey legend, holding a banquet in his honour.

Dave the mechanic, remembered it well, for in that skit we told Jerry and Norton to look at the head table to see who was there. Darryl smiled. The evening honoured him after all, and all the well-deserved attention was indicative of that. Sitting beside Darryl was the main organizer for the evening, Carl Buschert, who had played small town hockey for years.

When Jerry and Norton looked at the head table, they got all excited and said stuff like: "Are you kidding me? You mean he's here in person? I can't believe I'm in the same room with him and breathing the same air. I mean, he's a hero and I've followed his stats for years. He's been on TV and in the newspapers, and there he is! Oh my, this is SO exciting! And to think we're here to see him!"

Darryl Sittler's smile got bigger—he was loving it! The "boys" went on and on extolling the virtues of this great hockey player and then finally looked at each other, paused and said together, "It's … Carl Buschert!"

"We were almost on the floor we were laughing so hard. We just couldn't stop!" Dave the mechanic said, laughing all over again.

David and I agree that this joke got the longest laugh of our career! The people were wiping tears from their eyes and holding their stomachs. We thought they would never stop laughing.

That had to be over 40 years ago, and yet this mechanic remembered it as if it were yesterday and said he'd retold this story many times.

How truly thankful we were to be able to bring this much joy to so many people with Jerry and Norton.

Is there something that you still laugh about when you remember it? It's good to take it out, dust it off, and relive that moment and have yourself a good laugh all over again.

David and Nancy in one of many lavish church productions.

Gotta Love My Husband

Therefore a man shall leave his father and mother and be joined to his wife, and they shall become one flesh. **Genesis 2:24**

I am married to a man who loves to watch the odometer on the car. He gets a real kick out of seeing numbers in sequence: 1-2-3-4-5, or 5-6-7-8-9 and the like. On the way home from work one evening, David noticed that our car odometer was about to turn over to 100,000 km. David came into the house all excited, got the video camera and insisted that we all had to climb into the car and go in and out of our long lane so we all could witness the momentous 100,000—and on our own property no less. Big celebration!

This same man who studies the odometer hardly ever looks at the gas gauge. He dislikes driving into the gas station, getting out, filling up, and paying, so our cars pretty much need to "cough" into each station. Thing is, he doesn't mind one bit.

One Saturday night when we were almost home, the "ding'" sounded on the gas gauge. We live about 20 minutes from the nearest gas station, and to my horror, I looked over and sure enough. Empty. I didn't exactly handle it well and wasn't too shy about saying so.

"So, shoot me. No ... wait. We have a length of rope in the garage that you can hang me with and that would be cheaper and less messy." Well, how can you stay mad at that? I laughed, but I did have great concern that we would not make it to church the next morning. He usually says, "Oh, we can go to Toronto and back on what's in the tank," but he knew that wouldn't fly this time. The next morning in the car, the "dings" became more insistent. Could they have spoken they would have said, "Hey Dummy. You need gas, and you need it right now!"

You will be happy to know that we did make it make it to a gas station and to church. This turned into a huge relief for me and I think David felt the same way.

Anyone else out there like David? Is it a guy thing? If the car is on 1/4 tank, I panic, but not my hubby. He believes it's good to go for a long time. One thing for sure—never a dull moment. And I can honestly say I wouldn't want to have it any other way.

My anxiety about the gas situation did nothing to help it. I lost sleep that night for absolutely nothing. I like how Jodi Picoult says it: "Anxiety's like a rocking chair. It gives you something to do, but it doesn't get you very far." It would be to our benefit to get to the place where we stop worrying over events that we have no control over. Here endeth the lesson. (Are you listening Nancy?)

Celebrating so many adventures together.

David and me renewing our vows for our 25th. Left to Right: Rev. Keith Parks, David, Me, Bernie Talbot on guitar and singing the Hawaiian Wedding Song.

Love Being a Hostess

Be hospitable to one another without grumbling. **1 Peter 4:9**

My childhood home was like Grand Central Station when relatives and friends visited. I loved when our house overflowed with laughter, singing, and joy. So, it seemed only natural that I wanted our boys to have the same experiences as I'd had. In fact, when we were drawing up the plans for our new home, we made sure it would be "company-friendly."

Every Sunday that we were not out ministering as The Seiling Family, we'd invite between 10 to15 people over for the noon meal after church. I had it all down pat. On Saturday evening I'd make the dessert and set the table. Early Sunday morning I would be in the kitchen browning a 10-pound roast and onions along with preparing potatoes and carrots to add in a large roasting pan. Then I would pop it in the oven. Finally, I'd make a large bowl of coleslaw and then we'd head out to church.

The aroma of a simmering roast hit us when we returned. Soon our guests would arrive. I'd make the gravy, add another vegetable, warm the rolls, and serve the food. Our guests would congregate in our large living room talking and laughing until David called everyone to come to the table. He would say grace, then we'd all begin passing bowls and platters of food and dig in.

I shall always treasure those times of great fun, fellowship, and sharing the bounty with which God had blessed us. It seemed a little sad when everyone left, but then my family would help with the cleanup. We realized that we were equally as blessed as those who sat around our table. The memories would never leave us.

Although not everyone had a large house for entertaining, it didn't matter. It was the company that counted. For a number of years, our church had a program called, Tea and Toast, where families would invite someone over after church on a Sunday evening. The food wasn't important. The heartwarming time getting to know someone else in a relaxed atmosphere took precedence. Reach out and you will be blessed.

"And the Rest of You are Angels"

For the LORD does not see as man sees; for man looks at the outward appearance, but the LORD looks at the heart."
1 Samuel 16:7b

Something happened to me in the Spring of 1992 that threw me for a loop. At the time I did not know why, but I began to experience extreme exhaustion which turned into low self-esteem.

When I heard that a travelling ministry was coming to our church and they required actors, I mustered the energy and signed up.

"Finally, here's something that I do well, and this will pull me out of this slump," I told David.

The day came when the team arrived at our church to hold auditions for various speaking parts in the play. When it was my turn to audition, I gave it my all. My friends said, "Oh Nancy, you are such a natural actor, you'll get in for sure." I acted humble, but figured they were right!

Before they handed out the speaking parts, the judges made an announcement. "If you don't get chosen to be an actor, please don't feel badly, because you can be an angel." I remember thinking, "Big deal. The angels are the ones who can't act." One by one, the roles were handed out with lots of cheers for the winners, but I never heard my name called. I then heard the dreaded words, "And the rest of you are angels." I couldn't believe my ears.

"Those of you with speaking parts, please memorize your lines," someone said, then they dismissed us all for a lunch break in the fellowship hall. The shock hit me like a ton of bricks. I couldn't move. All I could do was watch while everyone else cleared out of the sanctuary. Finally, I dragged myself out and ran to the basement bathroom, sat on the floor by the toilet in the far stall and sobbed. "God. You don't love me. Don't you know how much I needed this?" Finally, I washed my face and went back upstairs to take my place in the angel section and did everything asked of me. The judges did give me the role of the head angel, but really, who cared?

David had been hired to videotape a wedding that day and we were also hired to provide the entertainment, so I had no choice but to attend. I cried all the way home, changed into my good clothes, and cried some more as I drove to the wedding reception. I didn't even try to apply makeup, for it would have been washed away with all the tears. When I walked into the hall, David took one look at me and knew something had transpired and it wasn't good. He led me to the car where I poured out my hurt and disappointment. All too quickly duty called, and even though I didn't want to, I knew that the show must go on. Soon we were making the rapt audience laugh. Only David knew my heartache.

I slept fitfully that night and the next morning I woke up still feeling depressed. After my shower, though, I heard God speak to my heart.

"Nancy, you do not have to perform for My love."

I suddenly felt His love wash over me. I shared this revelation with David and told him how I felt free, light, and happy from that moment on. I even found myself enjoying my angel role so much that some of the congregation came up to me after the performance to tell me that my face shone.

This turning point in my attitude marked an important moment in my life as I realized that God loved me just as I was. I no longer had to work for His approval. Shortly after that, I would be diagnosed with a debilitating health issue and would spend many long years in quiet seclusion. Had I not had the revelation earlier that year, I would not have been able to cope.

"Peace takes our hands off the controls and allows our Sovereign God to reign and manage and heal and repair. He does the work, and we step into His peace while He does it." Kay Jantzi.

I like that.

Dark Clouds Rising

Likewise the Spirit also helps in our weaknesses. For we do not know what we should pray for as we ought, but the Spirit Himself makes intercession for us with groanings which cannot be uttered.
Romans 8:26

Much to my dismay, fatigue began to plague me with greater intensity as time went on. It became a huge chore to have company. Even though it was wonderful, it was exhausting. I would remain in bed the next day trying to recover. I kept thinking that I must have been lazy and would push myself to do more and more to prove that I wasn't.

It all came to a head in August 1992. We were invited to be the children's leaders at a church camp in Northern Ontario. I had spent countless hours preparing. To our dismay, we found out that we were to begin the children's program 30 minutes before adult church started to "help the parents." This came as a shock and, looking back, I should have insisted that the children come at the same time the parents attended their service, but I meekly prepared even more material to put in the extra time. Some parents visited with their friends long after the service ended, and we had to wait until they came to pick up the younger ones. David and the boys had games and physical exercise outside for them each day, so I used this time to recover some energy. To be fair, the kids were well behaved and thoroughly enjoyed the sessions but the word "exhausted" didn't even begin to describe how I felt after each session.

The Sunday after camp, we were invited to another church for an open session Sunday School (children and adults together). I remember sitting in the front pew looking at the three steps to the platform and thought, "How am I going to make it up those steps?" Forget the fact that we had a 40-minute program ahead of us; my concern centred on how I would have the energy to climb those steps. Somehow, I made it through, but after that, my body shut down even more. I found that I was constantly climbing into bed during the day. I would drag myself out to do chores or prepare meals and then I would fall back to bed again. This horrified me and eventually I couldn't drag myself out any longer. I stayed in bed like a zombie.

I went to my doctor and explained my symptoms. "Are you depressed?" he asked.

"Well, I certainly am not thrilled! The fatigue is overwhelming." He sent me for some tests, but they all came back negative. I cried, not because I wanted it to be serious, but I had to know why I was tired beyond reason. I said to David, "Call it the Ding-Dong Disease, but please, give it a name!"

Nothing I did helped and one day I forced myself out of bed to see my Naturopath. I hoped he could determine the cause of my debilitating symptoms. He listened carefully and then asked for a urine sample. When he stuck the strip in, every square lit up like a Christmas tree.

"Nancy, you are one sick girl!" he said with great concern. "You mean there's a reason I'm so exhausted?" I asked hopefully. "Nancy, your body is screaming, and I hardly know where to begin, but I will do my best to help."

He asked to me fill out a questionnaire after a few weeks. "Nancy, I hate to say this, but I believe you have Chronic Fatigue Syndrome."

Yuppie Disease, a derogatory term for chronic fatigue syndrome. I couldn't accept it. However, the more I learned about it, the more I realized that, yes indeed, that was what I had. At least it had nothing to do with being lazy but was a serious health issue.

Have you ever had a diagnosis that took you by surprise? How did you cope? Were you like me—glad to have a name put to the problem, or did it make it worse? I like this quote: "In God's economy, you will never know which experiences will prove invaluable down the road." Kathy Herman. So true.

Big Adjustments

The LORD is my shepherd; I shall not want. He makes me to lie down in green pastures; He leads me beside the still waters. **Psalm 23:1-2**

The news that I now had a name for my crippling health issue, Chronic Fatigue Syndrome (CFS), helped, but it still seemed like an insurmountable challenge. At first, I had great trouble concentrating on anything and mostly stayed at home.

After a few months of extreme fatigue, crying in bed, and feeling as if I had hit bottom, I heard God speak to my heart once again.

"Nancy, you are My beloved." I cried even harder. "But God, don't you see me? I can't even take care of my family. Nancy has ceased to exist." God whispered again. "Nancy, you are My beloved."

At that moment, I experienced another revelation from God. I realized that although I spent most of the day and night in bed, He still cherished and treasured me. I felt His unconditional love pour over me like warm oil and I knew that all was well. I still have tears whenever I tell this story and am crying even as I write this. God's love proved very real to me when I remembered, once again, that I didn't need to earn His approval. He loved me no matter what.

As the naturopathic remedies helped, I discovered I could sit in bed propped with pillows as I read and studied for short periods of time. I had my Bible, my journal, and one or two devotionals, plus coloured pens, a highlighter, and a ruler to underline important verses. The Bible came alive to me and I copied good quotes into the wide margins and made notations of my own with dates. Each day I felt a wee bit stronger and could study for longer periods of time. I rejoiced when I felt strong enough to sit in my lazy-boy chair in the bedroom. Sometimes I'd light a candle and just stare at the dripping wax. I prayed or meditated. I felt peaceful during these hours and became conscious that I was sitting at the Master's feet. As I read and prayed, I realized that I had an Audience of One and that One became all important more and more as the days progressed. After a couple of years upstairs, I found that I could go down into the living room and sit in front of the roaring fireplace in the winter. My time with Jesus became glorious because I had little energy to do anything else. I had the luxury of taking as much time as I wanted.

How thankful I am that God showed me just how much he loved me. Not because of my performance, but just because I am His daughter. Do you ever feel that you need to work for God's approval? Hopefully, you won't need to have something happen for God to show you how much He loves you. I guess I needed a two by four plank upside the head!

Two years before CFS diagnosis. Left to Right: Jane, me, Janet

So glad I didn't know what was ahead.

My Quiet Years

Be still, and know that I am God; ... **Psalm 46:10a**

David and the boys were good to me during my bout with CFS and took up the slack. They never complained that I wasn't there for them. As a result, they became admirably self-sufficient. Nathan and Matthew were both in high school so they could take care of themselves. It also helped that some women from our church would make sure there were homemade meals in the freezer at church, which David brought home Sunday after Sunday. I felt loved and cherished.

I couldn't always go to church because of fatigue, but I do recall one time in the dead of winter deciding that I would try to attend with my family. My mom had loaned me her warm, long brown winter coat because she knew I felt cold all the time. After the service, I stood in a corner near the door and watched as the special guest speaker and his gorgeous wife walked by. I compared myself to them. The voices in my head were at it again. "Nancy, you are nothing but a small brown mouse and you will never be on stage or even be able to work for God again. Your life as you knew it is finished." This of course did not come from God, but still, it troubled me greatly. I had to work hard not to dwell on it.

The good news, though, I started to grow in my spiritual walk with Christ. My Bible was heavily marked. I could not get enough of God's Word and the Lord stirred my heart to read excellent commentaries. Slowly but surely, God revealed many of the misconceptions I had of Him and of myself. I saw how I felt driven to succeed and always seemed to find something I did wrong or could have done better after every performance. No wonder my body finally gave out!

All this time my husband, David, was very patient with me, even when he, too, experienced some rough waters. He'd been laid off as a salesman and draftsman for a store fixture company due to the bad economy. Not an easy time for a man in his 40s without a job prospect in the near future and with a sick wife at home.

One day, David, intrigued, followed up with an opportunity he had read about in the paper. The Government was offering a free course in Computer Aid Design (CAD). He signed up, even though we did not own a computer, and drove almost an hour each way to attend classes at the community college. Most of his classmates were much younger and had experience with computers. Because we didn't own a computer, David would stay as long as he could after hours so he could practice what he'd learned on the school's computers. He got good grades, but all the while his concern for me being alone gnawed at him. He soon realized spending so many extra hours at school wasn't working, and he reluctantly purchased a computer even though we couldn't really afford it. We were so proud of him, though. When he graduated, he secured a good job which eased his heavy load and helped us financially. We rejoiced at the goodness of God.

"Hold on to the good and leave the mystery of life's battles and question marks in God's hands." Margaret Jensen.

Wise words.

Just a Closer Walk With Thee

Therefore we do not lose heart. Even though our outward man is perishing, yet the inward man is being renewed day by day.
2 Corinthians 4:16

During those long years of dealing with CFS, I filled journal after journal with my thoughts and anxieties. Early on, I decided to write each entry as a prayer, and held nothing back. There were some days when I became so sick and tired of being sick and tired.

"How long must this go on God?" I begged.

But then, there were other times when I'd be at peace and could thank God for the countless hours I was able to sit at His feet and discover more about Him. And about myself. I found that I loved writing encouragement cards to those I knew who struggled, too. It was like music to my ears if I heard that my card came at just the right time.

Our boys flourished, and each graduated from high school and found good jobs. Nathan soon met the love of his life, Tanya, and they had a beautiful wedding. I had to sit on a high stool in the receiving line and felt exhausted after, but oh, what joy we experienced being part of their big day.

David and I were immensely proud when we became grandparents of their children, Samara and later our grandson, Taylor. They indeed brightened our world. I simply adored them both—and still do!

Even during trials, there are still times of refreshing. It is important not to just look at the negative but to see many blessings along the way. There is a Madame Blueberry (*Veggie Tales*) quote I love: "A thankful heart is a happy heart." I have found that this is altogether true!

Nathan and Tanya's beautiful wedding, 1997.

Compelling Vision

Do you not know that those who run in a race all run, but one receives the prize? Run in such a way that you may obtain it.
1 Corinthians 9:24

Around the same time as Nathan and Tanya's wedding, I had some people tell me that my problem was depression and if I'd only take a certain drug, I would be well. I would hear reports of their situations and how much better they were feeling. I thought perhaps the answer stared me in the face. I immediately began praying about it, but distinctly felt God press words upon my heart.

"No Nancy. It may be right for them, but that is not My plan for you."

This devastated me and I cried, feeling like God loved others more than He loved me.

However, God graciously gave me a vision. I know that it had to be a vision because it is just as vivid today as it was decades ago. Besides, I could never have made it up on my own.

I happened to be alone in the living room gazing at the bright flames in the fireplace when suddenly I "saw" two separate pictures side by side. The image on the right, a wide, paved road with a sign on an archway with flashing lights and the name of the drug that helped many others, beckoned me to follow. It offered a bright road to joy and above all, the energy that I so desperately needed.

The road on the left, appeared as a little gravel road. The sign on this arch above simply read, "God's Will" in wrought iron. Not only was it not lit up, but on the other side it looked like a sharp curve to the right, so I had no idea what could have been ahead. I looked longingly at the bright, paved road that promised me so much, then back to the small, darker road with the immediate bend signifying "God's will." It took me a while, but gradually, with tears coursing down my cheeks, I relented.

"God, I have no idea what will happen if I go on the road that says Your will, but I choose that."

I'd like to say things changed immediately but they didn't. In fact, those who suggested I speak to my doctor about medication were upset with me and made cruel assumptions.

"If you don't take this drug, you want to be sick!"

This of course could not have been further from the truth. As an extravert who loved being with people and enjoyed the interaction, this statement crushed me. I continued to journal all my hurt and disappointments, holding nothing back. I knew in my heart that I had made the right choice. David supported my decision and I decided I would carry on with the way things were.

Sometimes people have the best intentions, but their advice just is not right. It can be difficult to go against their heart-felt concern, but we also must do what we feel is best. If you are in a situation right now where others are telling you something that you do not feel is in your best interest, you may want to follow your instincts. It could be difficult but ask God to show you what is best.

Laugh or Cry

He will yet fill your mouth with laughing, And your lips with rejoicing. **Job 8:21**

As the years went on, it pleased me to be able to do more and more—but with caution. There were good days and bad days, so when the good days came, I rejoiced.

A man from our church died and, because I started to feel better, I called Janet and asked her if she would accompany me to the funeral. She seemed pleased that I wanted to go, so we agreed to meet for a quick lunch beforehand. Knowing how easily I still sometimes got confused she told me to get out a pen and paper and she would give me the details.

"Now write this down because otherwise you'll forget."

I asked Nathan to get me a piece of paper from the recycle pile and he brought a HUGE envelope and wrote in big letters, "Meet Janet at the corner of King and Columbia at 12:00." I took it along and held it up for Janet to see when she walked into the restaurant and we both laughed. After we ate, Janet took the big note from me, threw it away, and with a smile said, "If you keep this, you're liable to come tomorrow and wonder where I am!" It sure felt good to be able to laugh at my problems for a change.

We drove together to the funeral home and met the son of the deceased who we hadn't seen in years. I introduced myself. "And this is David," as I pointed to Janet. Of course, we laughed. We then had to sit at the front of the chapel because the rest of the chairs were taken (big mistake). We were singing a song with the word "heart" and Janet sang "tart." I tried not to laugh but my shoulders were shaking while I desperately tried to control myself. A bit later, Janet got another word wrong and I leaned over and said, "Read much?" She returned with, "Shut up, I don't have my glasses." This sent us into more muffled laughter much to our embarrassment, but when you get the giggles it's really hard to stop.

Pastor Marshall led the service and thought something must be wrong because of how we were acting. He looked down at his clothes to make sure everything was closed that should have been.

He then realized that we weren't looking at him or each other, so it must have been just The Dubrick Sisters acting silly.

Later he said, "The next funeral I lead, I'm going to separate you two because you're deadly together!"

Doesn't it feel good to laugh? Sometimes, we must remember that life is not all doom and gloom, so it's okay to lighten up. If we can laugh at ourselves it's even better and we will likely give others around us a good laugh, too. But preferably not at funerals!

One of my better days at our home with Mom and Ken and my sisters.

St. Kitts

But sanctify the Lord God in your hearts, and always be ready to give a defense to everyone who asks you a reason for the hope that is in you, with meekness and fear; **1 Peter 3:15**

One Thursday, just before Christmas, our minister, Pastor Keith, called David at work and asked, "How would you like to go to St. Kitts?" He explained that a pastor of a church on that beautiful island, needed a replacement Pastor. The regular Pastor had booked an intern to take over the church for ten days, but he had backed out so the family, disappointed they couldn't go home for Christmas, had contacted Pastor Keith, who immediately thought of us.

David shared his news with me and then we talked to our teenage boys. They agreed it would be an adventure. We quickly made arrangements to fly out in two days. What a whirlwind to get ready, but we made it and soon we were living in the Pastor's home, driving his car, and taking over his church.

St. Kitts was a gorgeous island, and the people were generally warm and welcoming. However, we were staying on the far side of the island where tourists don't often venture, in a little village called, "Half Way Tree." We had to wonder what caused someone to name the village such a name and thought it unique.

We were in charge of many church services and, before long, the congregation held David in high esteem as their interim Pastor. We did our best and we even brought some of our children's stories and some puppets to entertain the children. This also delighted the adults.

Occasionally, the lights would go out, but no one seemed to mind. We'd hear a shuffling and then some lanterns would be lit. A few times a dog or two would wander in through the open door and lay down in the aisle and no one thought anything about it.

We did notice that most people were casual in their manner and did everything with a slow, carefree attitude. However, put them in a car and it became the Indy 500! It didn't help that they had right-hand drive, so it made it all the more tense for us. David finally made me sit in the back seat when we were on the road, because I couldn't adjust to everyone being on the wrong side of the road. "David, Look Out!"

Our adventures continued, but on Christmas Day when I phoned home and spoke to some of the family, I had a good cry when the conversation ended. It hurt to be away from extended family over Christmas, but I soon got over it.

Because we were the only white folk in the village, we felt some tension, and we could feel eyes on us whenever we walked in the neighbourhood. We started to understand racial prejudice a bit more and it was not pleasant.

Our time in St. Kitts definitely turned into a unique experience and we were honoured to be entrusted with such a great responsibility.

It wasn't our typical Christmas, but it sure was amusing to see the children sliding down the long grass on the hillside with flat cardboard "toboggans." Even typically slow Christmas carols were sung with a Calypso beat. That was fun.

Are you the type who can handle an adventure on short notice? Not everyone can, but we certainly made a lot of memories as a family that Christmas. Sometimes, it is worth it by going out of our comfort zone, so go ahead and take the occasional risk. It just may work out for you, like it did for us.

David clowning around an old fort in St. Kitts.

Seoul, South Korea

You, O LORD, remain forever; Your throne from generation to generation. **Lamentations 5:19**

One day, a few years after our St. Kitt's adventure, we received a phone call from a Canadian missionary couple who were teaching in Seoul, South Korea. The wife asked if David and I would be willing to come to their International School and oversee four days of assemblies. Her mother lived in Drayton. She had seen us at a program and suggested her daughter should contact us.

This lady told us about the expectations. We would have to do the same program three times each day, but the third session would only have a moral message rather than a Christian one. She said she'd give us time to think about it. I told David about the call.

"Of course, we can't do it," I said.

"Why not?" David asked.

"Because we're not good enough." With that, David got upset and said, "Of course we're good enough! We've been asked to appear on the 100 Huntley Street TV program on a number of occasions. What makes you think we're not good enough?"

We ended up sending a tape of one of our programs. The people in charge were pleased with what they saw and before we knew it, we were booked to fly to Korea. Much of our luggage held our puppets and all the materials we'd need for so many sessions and it proved to be most interesting. The children that are accepted into these International Schools have parents who are diplomats or high-level government employees and must have at least two passports. We were amazed to see many of the children were driven to school in limos with chauffeurs. Such a different world!

Our programs were well accepted, and we thoroughly enjoyed spending recess with them each day. David had some card tricks that delighted the children, plus we would join in on the sports. We quickly learned to love these charming children.

Each day was long and tiring, but we were honoured to be asked to be the special guests. We found it difficult to finally have to say goodbye, knowing that we probably would never see these children again. Even if we came back in a few years, they all would have graduated.

We were able to do some sightseeing while we were there and learned much about the Korean culture. We walked through a huge museum and were given a tour by a retired general from the South Korean army. He told us how American and Canadian forces turned the tide against the communists and thanked us profusely, simply because of our nationality.

Occasionally, we'd have to pinch ourselves to realize we were in Seoul, South Korea, and we praised God for this amazing opportunity. He gave me the energy I needed, but I collapsed when we got home to Canada. The trip turned out to be well worth it and we prayed that we would meet those dear students in Heaven one day.

It truly is interesting to see other countries. If you get a chance, make sure you delve deeply into the out-of-the-way places that tourists usually ignore. You will be so glad you did, and you will get to see and enjoy the real culture that way.

My Favourite Job

And whatever you do in word or deed, do all in the name of the Lord Jesus, giving thanks to God the Father through Him.
Colossians 3:17

A friend of mine from church told me about her position as an escort for a tour bus company. At first, I thought she was joking when she called herself an "escort" but that was the correct designation and she shared how much she enjoyed it.

"Oh Betty, that would be like a dream job for me!" I gushed and meant it.

Because she was such a good friend, she asked the company if they needed any more escorts. It turned out, they did! I passed the interview and on my first trip I travelled with a seasoned escort for training. My new adventure began.

Oh, how I loved my passengers. I'd make all kinds of chocolate suckers and goodies to give out as prizes for the many games I'd planned for my passengers. On one trip to Niagara Falls I asked, "Who has been here before?" Hands flew up. Then I asked, "How long ago were you here?"

Different ones called out the years and then one woman proudly admitted. "My husband and I honeymooned here over 60 years ago." She won the prize! It happened to be a little chocolate "jewelry box" and she loved it. On another trip a few weeks later, a woman asked if I was the escort who gave an older lady a chocolate jewelry box. I told her I was.

"My mother has treasured that box ever since you gave it to her. It has a prominent place in her home, and she tells the story to whoever stops by." That certainly made me feel good to hear how much that meant.

One of the things an escort must learn is how to have "sea legs" when the bus is moving. Sometimes I liked to visit my passengers during the trip, and they seemed to like it too. On one trip when I had made it half-way down the aisle, the bus swerved, and I almost landed in an older Mennonite man's lap. Embarrassed, I apologized, but he only smiled and said, "Oh, that's O.K." I think he rather liked it!

The organizer had scheduled another trip to New York City on October 11, 2001, one month after the 9/11 terrorist attacks. The managers were in a quandary as to whether the trip should be cancelled or not. Eventually, they decided to allow the passengers to choose. Most of them bravely stated they would like to take the chance and the trip went as planned. The devastation was indescribable. Thick ash remained everywhere. When we were at the top of the Empire State building one evening, we could see the workers at the twin towers site with huge cranes and lights, still searching for bodies. No one said a word. Silence prevailed.

Some kindly New Yorkers thanked us for coming; many tours had been cancelled. A trip none of us will ever forget.

Being a tour guide and escort turned out to be my favourite job. I often think of those days with great fondness.

Can you remember when the twin towers went down on September 11, 2001? It seems most of us remember exactly where we were when we heard the news. This reinforces the fact that none of us knows when our lives will end. How important it is to live right so there are no regrets when we leave this earth.

An Exciting Opportunity

Jesus answered and said to him, "What I am doing you do not understand now, but you will know after this." **John 13:7**

My job as an escort was only part-time. One day while sitting on a bench outside a store, waiting for David to run some errands, I saw a beautiful motorhome drive by. The Lord seemed to say, "I'm going to give you a ministry where you'll be travelling in a motorhome like this one." I became excited and happily told David about it. Of course, neither one of us knew if I really heard from God, nor did we have a clue as to how or when it would happen, but I kept it close to my heart.

At this time, our church grew under Pastor Keith and Anita's leadership and eventually our choir had more members than some churches. Keith had written a series of books called, *Seeds for new Believers* and it soon became well accepted around the world.

A member of our church, Heather Card, who is a chartered accountant, felt impressed to write a children's version of *Seeds*. She approached Pastor Keith to ask him if she could begin writing it. He was skeptical until she told him the name—*Seedlings*. He then knew this came from God. Heather worked on it for a few years and found a young man, Jason Boettger, to draw fantastic illustrations to accompany her words. Once *Seedlings* was published, God laid it on Pastor Keith's heart to quit his position at our church and begin spreading this little booklet to many schools around the world. Pastor Keith admits to arguing with God at first, but then gave in. We were all heartbroken that he and his family would be leaving us, but we understood. In a short time, schoolteachers and missionaries were asking for this wonderful workbook for their school children. *Seedlings* had sprouted.

During this time, Pastor Keith's son, Reg, took his parents to a fund-raising travelling dinner-theatre.

"Dad, I can do this for Seedlings." Reg is an actor and a playwright who wrote an amazing play called, "Little One." They found four of the six actors and a tech crew of four, but they needed a manager. Keith said, "I know the perfect couple to be actors and managers."

Reg contacted us by phone, and instantly we knew that we were meant to be part of the team of 10. Through a series of long-distance calls, we met the other team members and just knew we were about to be part of something amazing. Although quitting my dream job hurt, this opportunity was too wonderful to pass up.

Remember the promise from God about how David and I would be involved in a ministry with a motorhome? Because we would be travelling full time across Canada, Reg and Keith knew that David and I would find it difficult to be billeted (meaning staying overnight in people's homes along the way,) so they let us use Keith and Anita's motorhome. The day it rolled into our driveway I knew instantly that it was God's voice speaking to my heart. My dream had become a reality.

Is there a vision that you are waiting to come to pass in your life? Perhaps you, at one time, have felt certain that God wants you to be in a different position, but it just isn't happening. It took over a decade of quiet solitude for God to get me ready for the challenge ahead. Be patient. God's timing is always best.

A Journey to Africa

For even the Son of Man did not come to be served, but to serve, and to give His life a ransom for many. **Mark 10:45**

Because our play for the dinner theatre was set in Africa, Keith and Reg felt that as the managers, David and I should go to Zambia, Africa, too. They planned to film the six actors who would often interact with the actors from Zambia on the huge screen. The screen would sometimes be used as a backdrop for indoor or outdoor scenes. At first, the audience would be consciously aware when we were speaking to the screen actors versus live actors, but after a while it just blended together.

David and I were glad we did go to Zambia, so we could see, first-hand, the great needs in that country. Our play centered around AIDS and the myth that if you have sex with a virgin, it will cure you of AIDS. The infected men tried anything to get rid of this horrible disease. One day David saw a picture of a little girl on a bus in Lusaka, Zambia with the caption, "Having sex with me will not cure you of AIDS."

In one of the scenes, the on-screen Zambian child actor is lying across her mother's grave sobbing, wondering what would become of her now that she would have to live with her mean Uncle. Reg got permission to film in a graveyard, but we needed two days to do it. Much to our horror, there were even more graves the next day. Apparently, there were often lineups at the gates with people waiting to bury their loved ones—most of whom died of AIDS-related illnesses.

We also spent five days in the jungle to learn how rural schools managed. Our guide showed our missionary driver how to get to each school. It always amazed us when out of the blue, we came to a clearing and in that clearing stood a mud schoolhouse. During our visits we would often serve the children a nutritious porridge-type meal called HEPS (High Energy Protein Supplement). The students' mothers would take turns cooking it daily in a large pot over an open fire. At noon, the children rushed to the cooking pot with their tin plates, cups, or even a large leaf for a plate, and sat down to eat. The expressions on their faces as they gobbled down the food indicated how much they loved it.

David brought a yo-yo and the children screamed with glee when he did tricks with it. They had no playground equipment and played catch with a rock. However, these children loved to sing and smiled brightly. They enjoyed the *Seedlings* workbook from which they learned more about Jesus. The teachers told us again and again how different the classrooms were when *Seedlings* was used as a resource. This impressed the teachers and the principals of each school.

We raised money to help print and distribute the Seedlings Workbook to children.

I had to smile when we were in Africa, because as a little girl, I feared that God would make me go to Africa as a missionary. Yet here I was with my husband and it turned into an amazing trip. We were able to make a passionate plea at each dinner theatre for ministry support overseas because of all we'd seen and heard in that beautiful yet troubled country. Many responded with big hearts and generous gifts.

"Grace is not opposed to effort but is opposed to earning. Earning is an attitude; effort is an action." Dallas Willard.

Makes perfect sense to me.

On the Road

> *But you be watchful in all things, endure afflictions, do the work of an evangelist, fulfill your ministry.* **2 Timothy 4:5**

We were amazed how quickly we bonded with our new team. Once we had returned from Africa, the rehearsals were long, and Reg proved to be quite the task master. But we learned much about the theatre: projecting to the back wall, blocking, stage right, stage left, upstage, downstage, staying in character, lines, and cues. So much to know!

David and I felt right at home in the motorhome that Seeds International had provided for us. I'd often pinch myself to make sure this was really happening. And to my delight, it was.

We were sent off on our adventure with much love and prayer by our many supporters. Six of us drove in the motorhome, and a pickup truck with driver and three other crew members pulled a huge trailer carrying all the equipment. (I don't mean the three other crew had to pull the huge trailer – they were actually inside the pickup that pulled the … oh, you know what I mean …)

Our debut performance happened in Mission, British Columbia. The meal and the play were well received. We knew we had an amazing story to tell and how excited we were, knowing many children would hear the Gospel because of our efforts.

When we had to move to each new venue, David would plan how long it would take to get to that town and would have the team's hosts bring them to our motorhome at the prescribed time. When we arrived at the new venue at noon, our hosts would have a meal waiting for us. We would enjoy some good food and fellowship then off to work we went. Step one meant unloading the large trailer. First thing to be unloaded was my kitchen box which had all the things needed for us to cook and serve the Zambian style meal. I began right away to sauté stewing beef and lots of onions. Once that cooked nice and brown, we put it in huge cookers, added cans of cubed tomatoes, and topped it with shredded cabbage, salt, and pepper. This would simmer for hours sending a delicious aroma throughout the building. Huge cookers of rice were filled, and we added rolls with butter and wafer cookies for dessert. All the food served in plastic bowls (made in Zambia) was so delicious that many asked for seconds and thirds. We even carried our own round tables with African motif lights. When the play began, the lights on each table dimmed. We had our own sound system and theatre lights, plus a huge screen with rear projection video to show the Zambian actors. Most people were wowed by this impressive production.

I could never have dreamed of this adventure on my own. Is there something you are dreaming? Keep praying. Keep believing. Consider this:

"I learned that I could not plan or even dream how God might want to do His work. My relationship to God was of supreme importance. I learned to love Him more dearly, to pray more faithfully, to trust Him fully, and to wait on Him with anticipation. When He was ready to use me, He would let me know." [*Anonymous*]

Humorous Theatre Antics

Beloved, let us love one another, for love is of God; and everyone who loves is born of God and knows God. **1 John 4:7**

Although travelling full time and constantly setting up the huge stage, lighting, sound, curtains, tables, and chairs, plus making the Zambian meal over and over again became exhausting, we also had fun.

Sometimes if we had time before the show, we would choose a video we all liked (especially a comedy) and watch it on the huge 8'x12' screen and laugh together. We also loved to play tricks on each other in front of and backstage.

In one scene in our play *Little One*, four of the six actors are in deck chairs feeling sad about the plight of young Namambo having to stay with her scary Uncle. Helpless, we could do nothing. At that point, another actor would bring us glasses of "lemonade" on a tray, which in reality were empty cups. One time, this actor filled them to the brim, and of course we weren't expecting it and spilled much of it on our costumes. We couldn't go out of character of course but had to complete the rest of the play with wet clothes and hoped the audience didn't notice.

In the same play we had two fine actors at different times portray the mean Uncle. Both Warren and Shambra were nice guys in person but the audience learned to despise them. We always warned the church or venue that this play was not for children, but sometimes the parents brought them anyway. One evening three girls were sitting close to the stage (something we tried to discourage) and right in Warren's sightline. The girl mouthed sadly, "Why are you so mean?" Of course, Warren couldn't go out of character, but had to tell us all backstage right away. From then on, we would often taunt him with, "Why are you so mean?" and dissolve into laughter.

One of the funniest things happened backstage. Three of the actors were on stage reciting their lines, and soon it would be my turn to join them. David and Warren were sitting in chairs and I was waiting in the wings for my cue. I looked back at David and threw him a kiss. At that instant, Warren reached in front of David and "stole" the kiss and kept it in his fist. David tried to open Warren's fist and they began wrestling. How hilarious! I couldn't help but laugh. It made it especially difficult that I had a serious scene coming up and had to swallow my laughter, change my expression, and walk out to deliver my lines. We talked about that often and it never failed to put us into gales of laughter.

It was times like those that kept us going. I'm sure every theatre actor has tons of stories to tell (and there would be some that we can't share).

"We can't blame other people for bringing out the worst in us because nothing can come out of us that's not already there to begin with." Karen Barber.

That's something to chew on.

Newspaper reporters often came to our dinner theatres.

[Photo Courtesy of Barrhead Leader. Sheri Lamb Photos]

Girls' Getaway

All the days of the afflicted are evil,
But he who is of a merry heart has a continual feast.
Proverbs 15:15

It was wonderful to be back home in between tours and to feel "normal" again. Each year, a few of my girlfriends and I got together at Lakeshore Church Camp for our "Girls' Getaway." On the second night we ate at a Chinese buffet and then walked to a Dollar Store next door to look around. I stopped at the dog toy section to get something for Nathan and Tanya's dog, Tyson. Nathan is particular about the squeaky toys because certain pitches bother his sensitive ears, so I started squeezing each toy to hear the noise it made. I came to a rubber chicken and gave it a good squeeze and heard a most embarrassing PFFFTTT sound. My one friend, Donna happened to be at the other end of the same long aisle and looked up. I motioned for her to come over and at first, she hesitated. (Poor thing probably thought she should wait until the air cleared.) She finally came over and I told her to squeeze the chicken. She did and we couldn't help but laugh at the obnoxious noise. One by one the five other girls heard us howling with laughter from different parts of the store and came to our aisle. Each one had the same reaction. There we were squeezing this dumb rubber chicken and laughing hilariously when the store clerk came toward us. We all thought "Oh-oh ... she's going to ask us to either step away from the chicken, or worse, ask us to leave the store for creating a ruckus." Instead, she said, "You need to try the pig!" We did try the pig and we all howled again. At the checkout, I said to the clerk, "Thank you for giving us such a good time at your store. This made our evening." I'm sure it made hers too.

We all agreed that we needed a good belly laugh and it continued throughout the three days that we were together. I can truly say, "And a good time was had by all."

Did something silly ever happen to you that tickled your funny bone? Did you give yourself permission to laugh? It's okay to laugh at something as dumb as a squeaky doggie toy in the Dollar Store or anything else that is too silly for words. Go forth and giggle. Spread a little joy and happiness. I double-dog-dare-ya!

Left to right: Anna, Donna, Greta, Nancy, Gloria, Anita, and Mary.

Meaningful Tour for Matthew

Take My yoke upon you and learn from Me, for I am gentle and lowly in heart, and you will find rest for your souls.
Matthew 11: 29

Over the seven tours in three and a half years that we were involved full time with the travelling dinner theatre, we had to memorize lines from four plays. The first one focused on Africa. The second play cast David as a tour guide for a trip to Rome with my "daughter." The sparks were supposed to fly between David and me and we made sure they did! We found it natural to flirt with each other which gave the audience lots of laughs.

The third play was set in Fiji and the scenes were stunning. In the fourth and final play, David and I were to be married in the first scene. I wore a wedding dress, walked down the aisle to my "groom" and the on-screen "minister" pronounced us husband and wife. When David welcomed the audience before the play started, he gave them a heads-up that this play would span three decades.

"This means you'll have to use your imagination to believe we're very young at the beginning." This always got a laugh. I had a long blonde wig for the wedding and transformed myself with different wigs and many costume changes. In one scene, I was supposed to be eight months pregnant with a pillow under my large top. Even though I made sure I had all our costumes laid out in order, it still became a challenge to get to the next scene on time. I often have nightmares that I'm unprepared backstage and wake up in a panic.

We were super pleased when our son Matthew was able to join us as our cook and bottle-washer for one tour. It turned out to be our favourite tour of all. Matt did a fabulous job.

God must have been smiling when Matthew came along, for it was on that tour that he met the love of his life, Sarah. One-and-a-half years later, we returned from another tour to attend their beautiful wedding. One never knows what will happen when we obey God's call—even if it's to be a cook and bottle-washer on a dinner theatre tour. Matthew and Sarah eventually gave us three gorgeous grandchildren and our family gatherings are sweet. I can't thank God enough for His many blessings.

I'm always amazed at how God works behind the scenes to make sure things happen. Matthew did not volunteer to come on tour with us to find a wife, but that is what happened. God is eagerly looking out for us, but He cannot force us to do anything. The important thing is to quietly listen and obey his voice, for His ways are always best. Just ask Matthew.

Matt and Sarah's beautiful wedding, 2006.

Matthew and Sarah

Hope deferred makes the heart sick, But when the desire comes, it is a tree of life. **Proverbs 13:12**

Even before Matthew and Sarah were married, they decided that they would like to have two children of their own and adopt one child. They had no idea if it would ever happen, but they kept this desire in their hearts over the years.

A year-and-a-half after they were married, they welcomed a beautiful baby girl and named her Launa. What a delightful child and so adorable. I loved to show her off in person or have pictures handy to share with anyone who would look at them.

Three years later, a bouncy baby boy came into our lives and they named him Trenton. Where Launa was quiet and methodical, Trenton came into the world and seemed to announce, "Here I am you lucky people!" We couldn't help but laugh at all his antics and Launa continued to be a wonderful big sister.

Matt and Sarah still felt the strong impression that a child out there needed to be adopted into their family. They decided to begin with fostering. The staff that approved foster parents were impressed with Matt and Sarah, and one said, "We wish we had more of your kind who would agree to foster." It didn't take long for a young girl named Breana to be placed in their home. Breana was a shy, sweet girl, who had been raised mostly by her grandmother because her parents were not able to take care of her. Almost immediately, Breana felt like part of the family and none of us could imagine life without her. It took a lot of hard work and patience, but the day came when her name was legally changed to "Breana Seiling." We couldn't have been happier to welcome her into our family and she remains very much our granddaughter.

Eventually Matt and Sarah purchased a beautiful piece of property near Ayr, Ontario and turned it into a family petting farm. They had two miniature horses, three sheep (who I called, The Dubrick Sisters), chickens, goats, bunnies, and ducks. The families that visited were delighted to observe what life on a little farm was like. David and I quietly watched them one Saturday as five families came at different times to enjoy the sights and sounds of the different animals. Our buttons were bursting as we observed the great job they did giving tours of all the pens, and ending the tour with a spot especially set up for family photos.

Life turned out better than they could have imagined, and they give all the praise and glory to God.

Is there something you feel you are supposed to do? It may not be as dramatic as adoption, but if there is a tugging in your heart, perhaps you should pursue it. You never know the blessings that could come out of your obedience.

Left to right: Launa, Matt, Breana, Trenton, Sarah. 2021.

Dump Story

Therefore, whatever you want men to do to you, do also to them, for this is the Law and the Prophets. Matthew 7:12

When was the last time you heard a good dump story? Well, in case it's been a while, I have one for you!

David and I were home for the summer, enjoying being back with family, and not having the responsibility of the travelling dinner theatre for a few weeks.

One day, Nathan and I were standing at the cardboard recycling bin at the town dump while his dog, Tyson, stayed in the truck. The windows were open because of the heat. Tyson started barking at another dog in the car beside us. I grew concerned and asked Nathan, "Do you think Tyson might jump out of the truck window?"

Nathan told me that it would not be the first time he jumped out. Apparently, the other time happened when Tyson was still a puppy.

"We were driving downtown Elora (population 7,980 happy people and two grumps) going about 40 kilometres per hour," Nathan said. "Somehow Tyson put his paw on the automatic window opener and the window opened." Nathan shook his head remembering how at the precise moment, Tyson spotted a squirrel and jumped out of the moving car.

"He did a face plant and by the time I got the car stopped, I saw that a woman behind me had parked her car sideways to stop traffic. I ran back to get my poor dazed dog who probably wondered what the heck just happened?"

As Nathan told his story, the woman standing beside us at the recycling bin gave us an odd look. She edged nearer.

"That was me!" she said.

Unbelievable! She just happened to be the one who stopped her car to stop traffic to help protect Tyson. And she just happened to be standing beside us at the dump as Nathan shared his story that day. We marvelled at the coincidence. We again thanked her profusely and went home with smiles on our faces.

So, how's that for a cool dump story?

We just never know who our angels will be in a crisis, or even if we'll ever see them again. It's important to be truly thankful when someone does assist us when we are in need, and to also watch for an opportunity to do the same for anyone in trouble. We can then return the favour.

Tyson as a puppy

Final Tour

Come to Me, all you who labor and are heavy laden, and I will give you rest. **Matthew 11:28**

Sometimes, for the dinner theatre, we didn't meet new recruits until rehearsals. To our chagrin, not all of them worked out well. It required a huge full time commitment from the cast and crew, and some could only take off work or school for one tour. This meant a high turnover. One tour turned out to be especially difficult, and it caused many sleepless nights for David and me. Not everyone shared their part of the workload, which meant the burden fell on us. But we had no choice but to carry on. Slowly but surely, we became more and more exhausted. Even our Christmas and summer breaks weren't rejuvenating us enough. Something had to change. Our families were concerned.

One stressful day, I grabbed the front of David's shirt.

"If I ever suggest we do this again, shoot me!" (and I meant it, well sort of.) Of course, there were many times we praised God for choosing us for this dynamic fundraiser and we did our best, but when exhaustion set in, even the smallest problem seemed insurmountable.

After six tours, David and I felt burned out and another manager needed to be found. We taught the new team all we could and sent them off with our blessing. However, it didn't turn out well, and Reg had to let the manager go. He asked us to come back to continue the tour. I really did not want to go back, but as we prayed about it, we knew that God wanted us to return. It took 100% obedience to say yes, but we were glad we did. The play that was underway only required five personnel, and two of the cast and crew stayed on. We hired a third person, and she did a great job. The ministry got back on track and we finished the tour on a high note, for which we were most thankful.

Just because one is in a ministry that is totally ordained of the Lord, does not mean there won't be trials and troubles. Are you in a difficult situation right now? Take heart. Our favourite saying when things were rough: "And it came to pass." Hang in there.

A New Ministry Opportunity

> *The LORD will guide you continually, And satisfy your soul in drought, And strengthen your bones; You shall be like a watered garden, And like a spring of water, whose waters do not fail.*
> **Isaiah 58:11**

David and I were enjoying our relatively quiet lives once we'd retired from the travelling dinner theatre. Saturdays found us happily searching for yard sales. David often bought, cleaned, and fixed bicycles he found along the way and sold them to three Old Order Mennonite men who had bicycle businesses. David cleaned the bikes so well that he'd even use a toothbrush to get into the cracks and crevices. He always added tongue-in-cheek, "but at the end of the day, I'd clean the toothbrush *real* good and give it back to Nancy!"

We were content, but still wondered if God had something else for us to do. We prayed about it, but nothing seemed to be on the horizon.

In the summer of 2014, we were invited to the cottage of our former Pastor Keith and his wife, Anita. The date they asked us to visit, happened to be our 41st anniversary which made it extra special. Their neighbors, George and Barb, were also friends of ours, so it seemed natural to visit with them. David sat on their deck fixing their son's bike and I ambled over. George asked, "Well Nanc', what's in your future?" I had to admit that there wasn't anything special.

"But you know George, I truly believe God has something big for us out there."

He leaned back and said, "I think I know what it is!" George went into the cottage and brought out some brochures for a charity that they'd been volunteering with for a couple of years. He raved about that amazing charity and how we would fit right in. As he spoke, something in my spirit leaped and I just knew this was meant to be. I took all the material he gave me, held it against my chest, and went into Keith and Anita's cottage and announced, "I think we're going to Hong Kong!"

As soon as we got home, we contacted the organization in Hong Kong and were sent a packet with questions that were so extensive that David said, "They forgot to ask what color underwear I have!"

The more we discovered about this charity, the more excited we became, and we greatly rejoiced when the staff approved our application. Immediately, we began looking into flights and started making arrangements to be there for six weeks. We weren't sure if we'd like it but decided that even if we didn't, we could survive for six weeks.

"When you are connected to God, your perspective is renewed, and your decision-making skills sharpen because you will be thinking more like God."[3]

---

[3] Farrel, Bill & Pam. Single Men Are Like Waffles. Single Women Are Like Spaghetti. Eugene, Oregon. 97402, Harvest House Publishers. 2002.

Joyful Anticipation

For I, the Lord your God, will hold your right hand, Saying to you, 'Fear not, I will help you.' **Isaiah 41:13**

As the time came closer for our departure, I became anxious. David and I were not sure we were up to flying halfway around the world to Hong Kong and then staying there for six weeks. We wondered what the accommodations would be like. I have severe allergies to molds and mildews and was most anxious about our accommodations. Had we truly heard from God that we were supposed to go? We'd prayed about it and did feel that yes, we were supposed to go, but what if we had been wrong? Although I did not obsess about it, I was weighed down with all the unknowns.

Three weeks before we left, I figured I had time to check out one last book from the library in Elmira. This little library had a large Christian section and I had found many good books there in the past. I finally chose one and began reading it as soon as I arrived home. To my surprise, the back part of a church bulletin slipped out. I assumed the person used it as a bookmark. What was written on the backside intrigued me. "Nancy. Joyful Anticipation." Suddenly I realized that this was a direct word from Heaven. God was personally telling me to stop agonizing over the choice we had made, and to look forward to it!

Only God knew who that Nancy was, and why the person wrote "Joyful Anticipation." Was it a note to herself, or for a gal named Nancy? Immediately, the burden lifted, and my attitude changed. God had planned that those three words be written on the back of that bulletin and placed in that library book. He made sure that this person returned the book in time for me to select it from the many choices. My heart sang.

Have you ever had a "coincidence" in your life that you knew was a "God incident?" When that happens, make sure you give the praise to God, for it is He who orchestrated it.

Hong Kong, Here We Come!

All the paths of the LORD are mercy and truth, To such as keep His covenant and His testimonies. **Psalm 25:10**

After much planning and many e-mails, we finally secured a date to fly to Hong Kong in February 2015. The staff at the charity looked forward to having us join them and soon we were on a long flight that seemed to never end.

The thrill we felt when George and Barb drove us inside the gates of this amazing charity filled us with wonder. It took a while to get used to the small apartment and the culture, but we found the excitement that the organization generated, contagious. The team welcomed us with open arms and we truly felt as if we belonged. Each morning we were eager to begin the day, and each night we fell into bed exhausted. As new recruits, we took orientation classes and were given tours of the huge compound. We learned a great deal in a short amount of time, and never stopped being in awe of what the charity did to help the downtrodden and those who endured untold agonies.

Soon we were absorbing Hong Kong culture on our days off and couldn't help bumping into people all day on the crowded streets (a most un-Canadian thing to do). We enjoyed many church services over the weeks with George, Barb, and their son, Peter, in downtown Hong Kong, then usually a delicious Chinese lunch would follow. After we ate, we had yet another taste of Hong Kong's many outdoor shops and markets. We shopped in an older indoor mall where many of the individual shops were about as big as most of our closets.

I now must brag about my one great accomplishment. Are you ready? (Drum roll please). I ate my Chinese food with real chopsticks. Hurray for Nancy! George and Barb suggested I buy toddler's training chopsticks the first weekend we were there, and I humbled myself to use them in a nice restaurant. They were bright pink with an "angry bird" on the top. I'm sure there were snickers behind my back, but I didn't care and now I can eat like a pro with adult ones. I had a little setback one time at lunch though when

George said "Ah, Nanc', your chopsticks are upside down." Sure enough, they were. That's what happens when I get proud.

Guess it is true that a haughty spirit comes before a fall. Humbled by my chopstick experience, I learned a lesson, plus it gives us something to laugh about. When was the last time you tried something new? If it's been a while, then go for it. You just might get good at it.

Time Flies

He who believes in Me, as the Scripture has said, out of his heart will flow rivers of living water." **John 7:38**

I didn't think time could ever pass as quickly as those six weeks did at the charity. We had adventure after adventure. We even visited Disneyland, Hong Kong with our new friends. I loved everything about the entire experience and felt like part of the family. I hated that the calendar sped full steam ahead. I desperately wanted to slow the clock down.

David and I became heavily involved in running programs to help people experience what it would be like to live in extreme poverty. People from all over the world came there to experience what it was like to live in the slums; to be blind for an hour in a totally blacked-out simulated African Village led by our blind guide; to walk in the shoes of four AIDS patients and hear their stories of how they contracted this dreaded disease; or become a refugee and feel the fear that millions experience every day when they are forcibly taken from their country and placed in internment camps.

I remembered how we thought six weeks would be long enough if we didn't like it, but when it came time for us to leave, I cried when the taxi drove out of the compound gates to take us to the airport. It almost broke my heart that our time was up. I could see our Chinese driver looking in his rear-view mirror wondering why this white lady was crying in his cab. I think it made him happy to get rid of us at the airport.

Even as we got on the plane to go back to Canada, we knew in our hearts we would be returning. Although we enjoyed being back with family and friends again, it took me a long time to get used to our quiet lifestyle. We deeply missed our new friends and thought of them constantly. Because they were 12 hours ahead of us, we looked at our watches and knew what they were doing at what hour. We longed to return some day.

It is amazing that God has a plan for each one of our lives. It may not be on a stage, or even in a foreign country. There are people right in your own neighbourhood who need you. The important thing is to listen and obey. God will take care of all the details if we stay close to Him and are open to His voice.

I Need Clean Clothes!

So then, my beloved brethren, let every man be swift to hear, slow to speak, slow to wrath; for the wrath of man does not produce the righteousness of God. **James 1:19-20**

I must admit that one of the things I eagerly looked forward to when we came home was to be able to wash our clothes in our own washer and dryer. When we were living in the compound in Hong Kong, washing our clothes had its challenges. The machines were often unavailable, but we wouldn't find that out until we got there. If they were full, that meant we'd have to keep making the long trek up and down a steep hill, each time hoping an empty machine would become available.

The first morning home, I put a load of wash into my washer and rejoiced at the ease of it all. My rejoicing soon turned to dismay when the silly thing wouldn't agitate. It filled up with water and then sat there like a mushy sack of potatoes. I pushed every button I could, but it would not budge. It seemed bad enough that we were dealing with serious jet lag, but when the washing machine wouldn't agitate it made me agitated. As a matter of fact, I grew agitated enough that it should have made the stupid thing turn! Why didn't it just ask me how to agitate? I could have taught it a thing or two about agitation!

David helped by removing all the sopping wet clothes and scooping the water out, but I wasn't handling it very well (to say the least.) David wasn't so impressed with the way I responded.

"Nancy, aren't you the one who said you have a new appreciation for all our blessings when you walked by the simulated slums every day at the charity? Yet now you're acting like this over such a silly thing."

Ugh. Silly thing, huh? Easy for him to say! He doesn't know how important it is for a woman to get her home (or nest if you will) back to normal again after a long trip away.

Actually, he is right. But ... (insert whiny voice) "I want my clothes clean!" We finally tossed it all in the car and headed to the nearest laundromat where we got the job done quickly. We didn't even have to climb a big hill or wait for a machine to become available. I am thankful. I am thankful. I am thankful.

Good news is that we did buy an excellent brand-new washer and dryer and I almost kissed the delivery guys when they brought it up. I did give them some homemade cookies and they appreciated the treat. All's well that ends well.

How do you react when things go wrong? Are you like me sometimes and whine and fuss, or do you just take things in stride? I must say that it is much easier on others and ourselves when we "go with the flow." I'll try to remember that when the next crisis comes.

Samara and Taylor

But the mercy of the LORD is from everlasting to everlasting On those who fear Him, And His righteousness to children's children.
Psalm 103:17

Grandchildren are a blessing from the Lord and ours are definitely delightful.

Samara was our first grandchild. Nathan and Tanya were living in the apartment above our garage but soon the time came for Tanya to return to work, so she needed to find someone to babysit Samara. I still suffered with Chronic Fatigue at that time, so Nathan and Tanya asked our Old Order Mennonite neighbour, Loreen, if she would consider taking Samara in. Their youngest daughter, Anna Mae, was Samara's age so it made sense. Soon Samara became a part of this wonderful household. We even found some "Anna Mae" dresses for Samara from the Mennonite thrift store and she fit right in. The two girls often played in the barn and sometimes Samara got to ride into town in the buggy and loved it. Although Anna Mae is now married, she and Samara are still bosom buddies and talk on the phone often. How thankful we were that this great opportunity opened up when it did.

Three years later, Nathan and Tanya presented us with a grandson. They named him Taylor and I adored him. Samara was a good big sister. With a family of four, the apartment was too small, so they moved into a townhouse in Waterloo and Tanya began her own home daycare. It worked well.

One Sunday, Taylor sat with us in church and tooted. He quietly announced this to me.

"O.K. Taylor," I whispered. I thought that would be the end of it. However, he proceeded to keep announcing it louder and louder. I had no idea how to get him to stop. Suddenly Tanya noticed what was going on and came to my rescue. She turned to Taylor and whispered, "What do you say?" "Scuse me!" he proudly answered, and immediately settled down. That's all it took, and from then on, I knew what to do. Such a simple solution. Why didn't I think of that?

While we were on tour, Nathan and Tanya had moved into the main house (with our permission, of course) and had moved our things into the apartment.

One of the pluses of this arrangement included me being able to watch Samara and Taylor get on the school bus every morning. I'd make sure to be at the window and would wave goodbye to them and always prayed for their safety, teachers, school, friends, and their future. What an honour. One morning I had to leave before the bus came and I discovered later that David put a wig on and took my place at the window. The kids thought Nana must have had a mighty rough night!

Over the years, Nathan and Tanya sometimes had to work late so I'd invite the kids up for supper and we'd often play games together.

One time when Samara was 11 and Taylor 7, we played a challenging card game called *Racko*. It took quite a bit of skill and the first time Taylor won, he was ecstatic. Suddenly David jumped up.

"Taylor, you cheatin' dog you!"

We all looked at David with shock, mouths agape. "It says on the box, *Age 8 to Adult*. You're only seven so you can't win. You're cheating!"

We couldn't stop laughing and to this day, we still chuckle about it. Samara and Taylor are adults now with lives of their own, but we will always have warm memories of our times together.

Not everyone has the blessing of family living nearby. If you don't, perhaps you can "adopt" someone into your hearts. It will make you both feel good.

Samara and Taylor, 2020.

Tanya's Surprise Birthday Party

For by me your days will be multiplied, And years of life will be added to you. **Proverbs 9:11**

One year, Nathan decided to give Tanya a surprise birthday party and sent out invitations on Facebook (blocking her account of course.)

David figured it would be funny to write Nathan this note: "We'd like to attend the surprise birthday party but need directions to your place."

Fact is, Nathan and Tanya live in the main house and David and I live in the apartment above the garage, so this was funny. Nathan, true to form, gave these instructions: "Go out your door. Turn right. Go down to the landing. Turn right. Walk past the garage. Turn right. Walk to our front door."

Not to be outdone, David wrote, "Words, words, words. I need a map!" Gotta love our family's humour.

Tanya thought Nathan was taking her out for a nice quiet dinner in Elora and was shocked when we were all in the back room yelling, "Surprise!" She truly was surprised because it wasn't that close to her birthday, so she suspected nothing. After saying goodbye, we all headed for Nathan and Tanya's and everyone parked their car on the other side of our large property in the country so they couldn't be seen from the road. Tanya again was surprised, and we all feasted on more food, cake, and ice cream and had a wonderful time.

The funny thing about Nathan and Tanya's birthdays is that they are six days apart. Nathan was past his due date, and Tanya came early, so Tanya is the "senior citizen" for six whole days according to our son. Nathan plays all kinds of tricks on her, like making a big show of assisting her in public and offering to get her a wheelchair or a walker. We all get a huge kick out of it. Once Nathan has his birthday however, Tanya isn't old anymore and everything is back to normal.

Oh. Just to let you know, we found our way back home without a map … even in the dark!

It's always fun when we can laugh at birthdays. Tanya is always a good sport and it makes it even better. Are you able to laugh at birthdays? If not, just remember that we only stop having birthdays when we die, so each birthday is special. That's worth remembering right?

Nathan and Tanya on vacation.

Imitation

Therefore be imitators of God as dear children. **Ephesians 5:1**

One summer David's former youth group from Bethel Mennonite Church had a reunion and, of course, we attended. I also knew many of David's friends, so we enjoyed catching up with all those who had moved away as well as those we'd lost touch with. Everyone seemed happy to be there.

Two ladies came up to me after lunch and after some small talk the one gal said, "I have something I have to confess to you, but I don't know if I should."

Of course, this had my attention and I encouraged her to share.

"For 10 years running, our family would attend a camp and at the campfire, my sister and I would pretend we were Jerry and Miss Nancy." I'd sit on my sister's knee and she'd pull on an invisible string on my back and I'd talk like Jerry. We'd even sing the duet *I Am So Happy* just like you and Jerry and the people would roar."

The other lady interjected, "We'd be laughing so hard we almost wet our pants." Year after year, the family would chant, "Jerry ... Jerry ... Jerry" and they'd do another skit. In fact, it became a tradition.

The first lady went on to tell me about her son. Apparently, once he got married, she didn't want her daughter-in-law to think she must be nuts so she quit, much to everyone's dismay. I begged them to show me their skit, but no amount of coaxing could get them to change their minds. I even suggested we go to the minister's office for a private show, but they wouldn't budge.

How glad I am that she shared this with me because, as the saying goes, "Imitation is the highest form of flattery," and this tickled me to no end. She made my day, my week, my month, and maybe my whole year! I just wish I could have witnessed their unique rendition.

Have you ever imitated someone? As long as it's in a positive way, let them know. It just may make their day, week, month, or year - same as it did for me!

Return to Hong Kong

Cause me to hear Your lovingkindness in the morning, For in You do I trust; Cause me to know the way in which I should walk, For I lift up my soul to You. **Psalm 143:8**

Much to our delight, later in that same year we felt God leading us to go back to Hong Kong; this time for six months. I hated to tell my mother the news, but she took it quite well. She and Ken were settled in their retirement home with all their needs looked after and she gave us her blessing. With great rejoicing we once again got on the plane in October 2015 for another long flight. The knowledge that every hour brought us closer to our destination kept us from going bonkers. We were thrilled when more friends from the charity were there at the airport to greet us. We talked the whole time about how things were going. They made sure to tell us how excited everyone was that we were returning so that lifted our weary spirits.

Because of our theatre experience, it didn't take long before the director and head of the simulation department (and the best public speaker we've ever heard) taught us how to facilitate some of these amazing productions where one doesn't just watch a play or listen to a speech but becomes part of the scenario. We were honoured to be part of such first-class simulations.

Here is an anonymous quote that I read somewhere that goes along with what our focus at the ministry was all about: "One of the most difficult things to give away is kindness; It usually comes back to you."

David and I with Hong Kong skyline in background, 2015.

Cute Charity Stories

Grace to you and peace from God our Father and the Lord Jesus Christ. **2 Thessalonians 1:2**

Much to our delight, the director gave David and me more and more opportunities to facilitate the different simulations. We were honoured that he trusted us to lead the groups that were booked, sometimes months in advance. Many times, we presented in front of powerful businessmen and women, sent there by their companies to learn about extreme poverty. We also enjoyed dealing with many groups of school children.

One of the simulations located outdoors in the simulated "slum village," offered an eye-opening experience for participants. Years ago, the charity built the village and added a well to get the message out that it took a lot of time and effort to get enough water each day to live. The child participants were lined up in groups, and each one held a five-gallon container of water for 10 seconds. Everyone seemed surprised to discover how heavy water was. Then they were given a chance to go into every "home" in the slums to see how millions of people must live each day. It was a sobering experience for these more privileged children to see the primitive conditions of some. It made them aware of how blessed they were. The children were also given pails to complete four "chores." Each time they travelled to the well (up a hill) and filled their bucket for four different chores, including helping to fill the community water barrel, fetching water to wash vegetables (rocks that look like potatoes), getting water to wash clothes, and the final bucket was to water the garden (no running or they had to start over.)

We always had question and answer times after every simulation. A boy from one of the wealthiest schools raised his hand and asked, "Does anyone live in these slums? I began to say, "No, these are only here for the simulations," when I realized he was pointing at the apartment building we lived in at the time. I laughed and said, "Yes, we live there!" Immediately I could see that he lost all respect for us for living in an apartment in such disrepair. To be fair, the inside looked in much better shape than the outside, but he didn't know that. Fact is, many companies offered to paint the buildings, but the leaders asked them to donate the money they would have spent on paint and labour to go towards the cost of shipping containers. Taking care of the poor seemed more important than our image.

Left to Right: David, Riba with baby Elias, Alice, DJ, Sherry, Erma, Nancy, Peko.

Another time, a Canadian teacher, working in Hong Kong, said that she made the mistake of telling her ultra-rich class that she had never flown first-class.

"There was a collective gasp from many of the students," she said, "because if Daddy didn't own a jet, they at least flew first class." She laughed when she said, "I don't think they ever glanced behind the curtain to see where most of the people on the plane would sit in cramped quarters."

Have you ever stopped to thank God that we only have to turn on a tap to have water? One of the questions we asked the children was: "How many taps do you have in your home?" Let me ask you that same question.

We have it so easy compared to many in the world and we never want to take it for granted. Next time you go for a drink of water, look up and say, "Thank You."

Difficult News from Home
But as for you, brethren, do not grow weary in doing good.
2 Thessalonians 3:13

A few weeks after we arrived for the second time at the charity, we received the message that David's father had died. He had been ill for a long time and we had hoped we would still be home when the time came. We found it difficult to visit him just before we left, knowing it would probably be the last time we'd see him on earth. He too sensed it would be our last goodbye.

My sister-in-law, Ruth, e-mailed me that Dad had passed peacefully with family around him, and I knew I would have to tell David when he walked in the door.

"Ruth wrote me about your dad, Honey."

That was all I needed to say. David saw it in my face and fell into my arms. We were in touch with the family, and they made sure the funeral was recorded on video. I wrote a eulogy and sent it to Nathan. He did an excellent job reading it at the funeral. Our hearts were with them all, but we had to carry on.

A dear couple from Zambia, Green and Christine, came to our flat the following day to give their condolences. We sat together in our living room and began talking about our trip to Zambia and our three and a half years with the travelling dinner theatre, created to raise funds for the school curriculum, *Seedlings*. David retrieved a copy of the curriculum from the office and showed it to Green and Christine. Christine hugged it against her chest,

"Green and I taught this in Zambia." We were stunned.

"You will never know the difference this little workbook has meant to teachers and to the children. The atmosphere in our school changed once we started teaching this to grade five students and now, we find out you helped raise much of the support for this. How can we ever thank you?"

There were hugs and tears and we stood in awe that God made sure that David and I from Canada, and Green and Christine from Zambia, would be working together in Hong Kong so we could be encouraged during a difficult time after losing David's father.

God turned our mourning into joy, and we gave Him the praise.

Even when things seem dark and we feel alone, God steps in and gives us encouragement. Trust God entirely, even when you do not understand what He is doing.

Left to right: Ronald, David, Dad, Terry, Jeffrey.

Philippines Break or What?

> *I beseech you therefore, brethren, by the mercies of God, that you present your bodies a living sacrifice, holy, acceptable to God, which is your reasonable service.* **Romans 12:1**

Because we did not have Hong Kong permanent resident status, our visas ran out after three months. We were required to leave the country for a while. The Lord had that all planned out, too. One of David's nephews, Greg, his wife, Sarah, and their family were missionaries in the Philippines. We made arrangements and took the short two-hour flight to their compound and spent a few days together. While we were there, we saw the work that Greg and Sarah were doing with boys that they rescued from the streets. The truly fortunate ones were taken in and given a place to live, fed nourishing food, and taught different skills including woodworking, auto shop, computer classes, and Bible studies. The boys thrived and many became respected and productive citizens when they graduated from the program.

Greg and Sarah also missed David's father's funeral, but someone had sent a DVD of the service to us, so after their children were in bed, we watched it together. It wasn't quite the same as being there, but it was a good quality recording, and we were touched by the loving tribute to a great man. We almost waved at our family as they filed out of the church at the end of the service for that's how real it seemed. We shed some tears but were pleased we could be together virtually, at least, to "attend" the service from a couple of months later and half-a-world away.

When we got back to the charity, David and I gathered as many things as we could find that Greg and Sarah would need at the compound and put it all in shipping containers. Clothes, shoes, books, stationary, and the most prized possession of all—computers. David was an excellent packer and wrapped each computer in the high-quality king-size bedsheets donated from five-star hotels to keep them safe. When Greg and Sarah opened the boxes in the Philippines, only one item had sustained a bit of damage. The women cried tears of joy when they saw all the fabric from the sheets. They would be able to make twin sheets, curtains, clothes, and whatever else they needed. To them, the fabric was pure gold. Greg and Sarah sent pictures of their new and improved computer room to us. The teachers and the boys were thrilled. What an honour to be involved in helping street kids have a better chance at life.

"With every sunrise we are presented a fresh, blank page in our life journal. The Lord is a God of new beginnings and He gives us the freedom to fill each page with whatever we choose." A. Jean Mott.

Good words to chew on.

Free Time

> *Now thanks be to God who always leads us in triumph in Christ, and through us diffuses the fragrance of His knowledge in every place.* **2 Corinthians 2:14**

One of the perks we enjoyed while in Hong Kong was visiting Disneyland. Both David and I, happy seniors, were able to get a season's pass for just a little more than one regular adult day pass. I loved Disneyland and felt like a kid skipping through those magical gates. All volunteers had Sundays and Mondays off, so many times, we took a bus, an underground, and finally boarded the Disney train that would take us into the grounds. We loved every second there and occasionally we would even be the tour guides for other visiting volunteers. We learned all the best spots to go and where to eat. Everyone had a terrific time.

Another highlight included the church we attended every Sunday. The services, held in an office building, made us feel right at home from the very first time we attended. We eagerly looked forward to each service and came to know and love many of the congregation and ministers.

Close to Valentine's Day the church offered all married couples a date-night and David and I were asked to be the speakers. The social committee turned the all-purpose room of the church into a thing of beauty. Red and white tablecloths, candles everywhere, delicious appetizers, main course, and scrumptious desserts were offered.

After the meal, David and I introduced a game where we gave each couple some paper and pencils and told them to separately (no peeking) write down their differences and then compare them. The couple with the most differences won a prize. David and I gave our differences as an example: He drives fast, I drive slowly. I am a neat-freak while David ... well, let's just say he's not! When the couples were finished their lists, we invited them to share. At first, no one moved, and we were worried it was going to fall flat. Soon a brave couple broke the ice and the others quickly followed suit until our stomachs ached from laughing so much. We then shared how differences were often healthy in a relationship. After all, if a couple agrees on everything, then one of them is not needed. We encouraged couples to look at their differences in a new light and to then celebrate rather than trying to make the other person conform.

Then David and I shared our courtship and marriage and had them almost on the floor laughing. Of course, there were tears too, but we wanted to give these couples a night they would never forget. We were pleased with the response.

All too soon the evening was over, and we reluctantly walked to our bus stop. David and I had never been in downtown Hong Kong at night before, so we were glued to the bus windows, drinking in all the bright lights and fancy displays. We had never seen anything quite like that before. Truly magical.

"Hold on to the good and leave the mystery of life's battles and question marks in God's hands." Margaret Jensen. Sound advice, I would say.

All Things Come to an End

Let not mercy and truth forsake you; Bind them around your neck, Write them on the tablet of your heart, And so find favor and high esteem In the sight of God and man. **Proverbs 3:3-4**

Things were going along smoothly until I came down with a terrible flu bug. I felt sick and miserable and longed to be home. Alas, I was half a world away. I struggled because I could see the beautiful cafe from our third story kitchen window and longed to be a part of the volunteer family rather than being laid up and segregated. I tried some of the pain medications from Hong Kong pharmacies but none of them seemed to help. David still worked while I rested in bed. One day, my doorbell rang and there at the door was one of the Canadian volunteers. He held a bottle of Tylenol and offered it to me. I could have cried, for Tylenol is my first choice when I have a cold or the flu. I began to feel more like myself and soon I felt like I was once again in the land of the living.

Every time long-term volunteers would leave, there would be a special party for them. It was always difficult to say goodbye. Each one had become like family and we are still in touch today with many of those beautiful people no matter where they live or serve in the world.

Finally, after six wonderful months, it was our turn to say goodbye. Someone had a beautiful idea to plan a huge bonfire in the Shire (as they called the large field) along with a singsong and sharing time. Our hearts were warmed more from the love than the fire and again, it proved difficult to say goodbye to our friends.

The morning before we flew out, we had another tearful goodbye. On one hand, I wanted to go back home to Canada to family and friends, but on the other hand, I hated to leave. We had no idea if we would be back, so once again, as we drove through the gates, my emotions felt ragged.

The flight home seemed to never end, but finally we were touching down at Toronto Airport. Nathan and Matthew were there to meet us. Nathan had a huge banner on the car, "I'm SO excited. My mommy and daddy are coming home!" He made it look like a child's writing and we roared. Oh, how good it felt to hug them again and talk all the way home.

The next day, we surprised our two youngest grandchildren by going to their school. As they filed out, their faces lit up as they flew into our arms. However, our four-year-old grandson, Trenton, pulled away and with an accusing finger looked at us and said, "I miss-ted you!" How precious those words were, and we had to laugh at his sincerity.

"Home sweet home." There is something special about coming home and know that we were missted! Whether it's long term or short term, treasure your family and friends when you return. We never know when any of us will no longer be around.

Never Hurts to Laugh

And you shall know the truth, and the truth shall make you free."
John 8:32

I'm not too sure if this is a "you had to be there" kind of story, but I've got to tell you what happened at our Naturopath's office shortly after we arrived home from Hong Kong.

Because Hong Kong had such high humidity, there were many molds and mildews. David had been in charge of tearing down some of the old shacks, and somehow a bug latched onto his lungs. The doctor there ordered x-rays to make sure it wasn't pneumonia, but thankfully the results had come back clear. We were relieved because we were due to fly home in a couple of days. We did make an appointment with our naturopath to have David checked out as soon as we arrived home though, and we were glad we did.

John listened to David's lungs and had him cough, etc. He then said, "David, if I didn't know better, I'd think you were a two-pack-a-day smoker. Oh no! Because David never smoked in his life, that was not a good prognosis.

John then pointed to his own throat.

"Do you feel a tickle here?" Of course, David knew what he meant, but said, "I don't know, John. It's your throat, so I can't tell if you have a tickle there or not!"

It took a second, but soon John and I were laughing at the joke. I think David needed a coping mechanism having just found out that his lungs were comparable to those of a chain-smoker. It certainly broke the tension. Then, John prescribed some drops, and the receptionist poked her head in the office.

"Is it the large drops or small drops?" Of course, she meant a large bottle or a small bottle, but David (still in a rare mood), said, "I don't think my throat can handle the large drops, so I'll take the small ones." This time neither John nor I got it, and his disappointment showed. On the way home, David said, "My throat can't handle the large drops. Get it Nancy?" Suddenly I did get it and had a good laugh.

The remedies that John prescribed took some time, but soon David's lungs sounded closer to normal and we were all pleased. We'll fondly remember how David's humour got us through a difficult time.

It isn't always easy to see a lighter side when given not-so-good-news, but it certainly made a difference to us that day in the office. We can't always choose what happens to us, but we can choose how we respond.

Jane's Release to Heaven

> *In My Father's house are many mansions; if it were not so, I would have told you. I go to prepare a place for you. And if I go and prepare a place for you, I will come again and receive you to Myself; that where I am, there you may be also.* **John 14:2-3**

Once again, David and I felt compelled to return to Hong Kong but this time for only three months. Mom agreed that she would be fine in her cute little room in St. Jacobs Place and she told us not to worry.

We were concerned before we left, because my younger sister, Jane, had been diagnosed with cancer. She had surgery and seemed to be doing fine, so we assured the family that if Jane took a turn for the worse, we would fly home early. Because Hong Kong is 12 hours ahead of Ontario time, we would be home the next day their time. We kept in close touch, but nothing changed. We again had a glorious time with our volunteer family. We thoroughly enjoyed the work and loved our time together but after three months, once again, we had to say another farewell.

Our plane touched down on March 27th at 7:30 p.m. Jane's life ebbed away exactly one month later on April 27, 2016 almost to the hour when we arrived back in Canada. She was only 59, but fully prepared to die knowing Heaven awaited. We spent much time with her in a beautiful hospice and often sang songs that we performed as The Dubrick Sisters and The Joyful Sound. Many times, people would thank us for the music that they heard through the closed door and we were thankful we could be a blessing to others. We were all by her side when she quietly breathed her last breath.

"What is she experiencing now?" I wondered, after Jane took her final breath.

We can only imagine the thrill of her walking through those gates of pearl, seeing Jesus, and falling at His feet in thankfulness. We'd like to believe that Daddy and our grandparents and others who had gone on before were there to welcome her home. Finally, pain-free, Jane could run, dance, sing, and shout once again. How glorious for her.

We may not understand the "why" of what we think of as an early death, but God does, and that makes all the difference. Someday God will change our question marks into exclamation marks, and everything will be crystal clear. Until then, we trust.

Jane left us far too soon. Miss her terribly.

Honduras Opportunity

Then He said to them, "The harvest truly is great, but the laborers are few; therefore pray the Lord of the harvest to send out laborers into His harvest. **Luke 10:2**

Our former Pastor and boss, Keith Parks, asked if David and I would be interested in going to Honduras with a team called Seeds and Socks. He told us we would be taking socks for each school child involved in our *Seedlings* curriculum. We knew the Canadian missionaries, Dale and Carolyn, so we agreed.

We didn't realize how much work it would be to buy thousands of pairs of socks and then package and mark them for boys or girls with the proper sizes. We had work teams set up in other churches and even travelled to help the volunteers and to pick up socks. One of the team members could not come up with their quota so it fell to us and we worked overtime to meet it. On top of it, we were asked to find gifts for the teachers that would be suitable but not too heavy because of the luggage weight restrictions on the plane.

The day came for us to leave Canada. Soon we were in Honduras. We were not pleased to discover that the place where we would be billeted although lovely, consisted of separate dorms for girls and boys. David and I hated to be separated but what could we do? Soon we found ourselves travelling from school to school, teaching lessons and handing out socks (there were two pair of socks in each packet) to each of the children.

You would have thought they'd won the lottery. People are greatly impoverished in many of the areas, but the missionaries are doing a good job to help those who need it the most. The children would almost topple Dale over when he walked through the gate because they were so happy to see him. Many of these children do not have fathers so he became both their father-figure and role model. What a sight to behold.

We were exhausted by the time we arrived home again, but it was a good exhaustion. We were glad we obeyed God's call.

"God's will done God's way, by God's appointed person(s), in God's timing will get God's results." Ron Smedley. Yes!

2017. Left to Right: George and Barb Grosshans, Nancy and David holding packages of socks for schoolchildren.

deCycles Staff

And whatever you do, do it heartily, as to the Lord and not to men, ... **Colossians 3:23**

David and I decided we would volunteer one final time as staff for deCycles. We were two weeks into the trip, spending the night in Asheville, North Carolina. Our overnight accommodations were in an old church that didn't have the best plumbing. With 60 plus people, it put a great strain on the system and there were problems.

Late one night, the girls were using the facilities upstairs and soon realized they were in trouble when water started backing up out of the drinking fountain. The staff was alerted. Bob put signs on all the bathrooms upstairs saying they were closed and to use the toilets downstairs. David carefully opened the main cleanout plug and as he prepared to unplug it, one of the girls flushed and it exploded! He tried to put the plug on again but— too late! His shirt was covered with you-know-what. "Oh crap!" His only comment.

David's red shirt was no longer red. so he figured he may as well stay with it and try to unclog the drain. He had limited success, so they decided to shut the girl's bathroom down using chains this time to be on the safe side.

All this time I slept on, oblivious of the drama unfolding.

David continued sharing the whole story the next day. "There I was, in the furnace room after suffering the indignities of the deluge. I had stripped down to wash myself along with my clothes in the janitor's big tub when one of the girls breezed through."

Horrified, I asked, "Who was it?"

"I don't know dear. I didn't take the time to wave to her!" David dryly replied.

The next day two staff members, Bob and Penny, and David and I headed to a local laundromat. As we tackled the large loads, we laughed at what David had experienced the night before. When we pulled the clothes out of the dryer, one piece had a tissue stuck to it. Bob pulled it off, and put it on David's chest and said, "Poomagnet." We were laughing so hard and for so long that I'm sure the owner wanted us out of there.

Such is the life of the deCycles. One never knows what will happen. But what stories.

"Experience is not what happens to you; it is about what you do with what happens to you." Aldous Huxley. Isn't that the truth?

Left to Right: Alyssa Houze (daughter), Norm Houze, Me, David, Cricket Houze, Daphne Houze (daughter). Norm and Cricket have been the Directors of deCycles Indiana since 1995.

Third Generation Ventriloquist

Only fear the LORD, and serve Him in truth with all your heart; for consider what great things He has done for you.
1 Samuel 12:24

Much to our delight, our nine-year-old granddaughter, Launa, showed an interest in ventriloquism. We happily gave her a girl puppet she named Lily Anne and taught her the basics of the craft. She caught on quickly and soon made her debut with us at a Seniors' luncheon in Waterloo. Her parents, Matt and Sarah, along with siblings, Breana and Trenton, sat in the front row to cheer her on. Although a bit nervous, Launa did a fantastic job and the crowd loved her. Right away we noticed that she had the "it" factor, so whenever we could, we would take her on our engagements.

Any performer will tell you that it is less challenging to stay with a memorized script, but to do impromptu, and do it well, cannot be taught. One time I asked Launa a question, but Lily Anne answered instead, "Why are you asking her? I do all the talking. She just stands there and holds me!" Everyone roared and we were most impressed that she came up with that on her own.

She's so good that it has gotten to the place where the people who book us for gigs specifically ask for Launa. Huh! What are we - chopped liver? Of course, we are super proud of Launa and she is gaining valuable experience in front of crowds and how to handle the accolades that come with being on stage.

Launa with Lily Anne has entered some talent contests. When she wins, that often means she gets to carry on to the next level. Our buttons are busting to have another generation carry on this unusual craft.

Talents are gifts, and we want to make sure and give the glory to whom it belongs—our Lord and Saviour, Jesus Christ. He blessed us with these abilities, and it is our desire that we use them to serve God in everything we do.

We all have gifts and talents. We are equally proud of Matt and Sarah's older daughter, Breana, who is a writer and our grandson,

Trenton, who is an excellent drummer. I come from a family of talented singers. Some may have more noticeable gifts and talents if it is in front of audiences, but the "behind the scenes" talents are just as important. Celebrate the gifts you have, no matter what they are and use them to the best of your abilities. You will be blessed as well.

David, Norton, Lily Anne, Launa, Jerry, Nancy.

Difficult Decisions

And the LORD, He is the One who goes before you. He will be with you, He will not leave you nor forsake you; do not fear nor be dismayed." **Deuteronomy 31:8**

In my first book "When is Tomorrow?" I share our long journey with Mom's dementia in detail, so I'll just give a brief overview. It became noticeable to us and the staff at St. Jacobs Place that Mom's mind was failing, and we struggled along with her. When dementia hit, she would be crying pitifully and would threaten to run away. The staff took this very seriously, for in a retirement home there are no locks on the doors, and anyone can leave on their own accord. Her threat to throw herself in the river nearby when dementia took over concerned the staff and they would call either my sister, Janet, or me to stay with her until her confusion passed. We hated to have to remove her from such a beautiful home, but the nurse gently mentioned to us one day that if a room opened up at Heritage House in long term care, we should take it. This was her kind way of saying that they couldn't be responsible for our mother any longer.

One day we got a call from Heritage House saying that a private room had opened up for Mom and they could take her right away. Janet, (our diplomat) gave the news to Mom in such a way that she actually began looking forward to it. We did have an ace in our hand we could play if we had to. Ken and Mom would be in separate rooms, but at least they would be together. We all knew that if they shared a room, Mom would completely wear herself out trying to take care of Ken. We assured her that his room was just down the hall so she could go there as often as she liked. Another plus turned out to be that her room overlooked the walkway to the front door and there were many trees and flowers. It passed the all-important "good view" test.

Things turned ugly after a couple of days however, and mom threatened to run away again. When she lived at St. Jacobs Place, we always came running when she uttered her threat but now, she was safe in a controlled-access facility. We knew she could not escape. However, when mom realized that her ploy to get us to come would not work anymore, she lamented that she was in prison. She begged us to take her back to St. Jacobs Place but of course we could do nothing about it. It broke our hearts.

Very few find it easy to make the decision to move a loved one into long term care. Janet and I couldn't give her the care that she needed but it still broke our hearts.

I like this quote from Margaret Jensen: "Hold on to the good and leave the mystery of life's battles and question marks in God's hands."

We must learn to trust God with unanswered questions.

My precious Mama.
Life hasn't been the same since she went Home to be with Jesus.

Mom's Release to her Heavenly Home

But as it is written: "Eye has not seen, nor ear heard, Nor have entered into the heart of man The things which God has prepared for those who love Him." **1 Corinthians 2:9**

Skip ahead two tumultuous years. Even though Mom faded quickly at the end, it still hurt. That evening when I got the call informing me that she may not make it through the night, I was over two hours away. But Janet stayed by her side until I arrived. It had been a long day for Janet, so I relieved her. Three hours later Mom simply stopped breathing and the Angels ushered her into the Presence of the Lord she had loved and served all her life.

Mom had given explicit instructions that her funeral should not be about her, but about Jesus. She wanted Janet and me to lead the whole service and to include a lot of singing. So, like obedient daughters we are, we did just that. I gave the eulogy and Hank, Janet, David, and I sang many of the songs we used to sing for her. Grandchildren read scripture verses, and some sang. Mom did not want us to grieve for her so David and I sang a meaningful song, "Celebrate Me Home." We felt that mom would have approved.

Now the mantle has been passed. Hank, Janet, David, and I are the *older* generation now. Our prayer is that we will finish just as well as Mom did.

We all know that in any race it is important to finish well. This race called life is no different. Each of us has our own journey, our own pain, happiness, and experiences, but our attitude is all important. Stay true to God. Hold on to what is good, and He will help you to finish well.

Final Goodbye

Have I not commanded you? Be strong and of good courage; do not be afraid, nor be dismayed, for the LORD your God is with you wherever you go." **Joshua 1:9**

When it came time to bury Mom's ashes, we had a simple ceremony with family. As per mom's wishes, there was no fancy urn; only a cardboard box just as she had requested. And now she is buried with our daddy and our sister, Jane. All are safely in Heaven with our precious Jesus. We were trying hard to imagine what it was like. Were Daddy, Jane, and Mom's parents, standing with Jesus at the gate to welcome her home? We would love to think so. However, it doesn't matter, for whatever she saw would be more glorious than we could have possibly imagined.

At the ceremony we continued to share memories of Mom. Hank, David, and Ross (Jane's husband) all agreed that they had the best mother-in-law ever. She never intruded in our lives, nor did she tell us how to raise our children, but she always pitched in to help us whenever she could. We did have to laugh when we recalled what she told each of her daughters before we got married: "Don't come crying home to me complaining about your life. You chose this man, and you work things out together and leave me out of it." We all knew she meant it, so we never even tried!

Mom never held a grudge and never had bitter feelings toward anyone. She had the ability to just love—even if they were unlovely. Whenever she became angry at Daddy (which didn't happen very often) she'd wait until he walked away and would stick her tongue out at him. Both Janet and I witnessed it on occasion and had to laugh because this served as a release valve for her. After that, her frustration lifted, and she carried on.

Mom had a huge heart. As long as she remained in the background working without fanfare, she managed well. Her emotions were on an even keel, while we three girls wavered between happy, sad, elated, or just plain moody. Our highs were high, and our lows were low, but not Mom. She was as steady as a rock.

Before we left the gravesite that day, we sang a song we'd often sung in Mom's room and one that we had sung at her Celebration of Life, "When I've Gone the Last Mile of the Way."[4] I wasn't a very good alto that day, for my voice cracked and tears stung my eyes, but I'm sure Mom didn't mind.

We knew that when she walked through those gates, Jesus, with open arms said, "Well done, good and faithful servant." We smiled at this because mom probably had a shocked look on her face when she heard those words and would have said, "Really? You think I did good?" A woman of true humility, she had a hard time accepting accolades and never thought she did anything special, nor did she feel she had any impact on her world. But in this case, she was mistaken!

Well done Mama. Well done.

I'm sure we all want to hear those words, "Well done." The first important act is to accept the truth that Jesus died for our sins and rose again from the dead. His death became the sacrifice needed and He took away all the sins of the world.

However, like any gift, it isn't ours until we receive it. Once we have accepted Christ as our Saviour, we will want to do everything we can to love God, love our neighbours as ourselves, and live the way He wants us to live. We cannot do this on our own, but we can with God's help.

---

[4] "The Last Mile of the Way." Author: Johnson Oatman, Jr. (1908); The New National Baptist Hymnal (21st Century Edition) #406,).

Funny David

I will bless the LORD at all times; His praise shall continually be in my mouth. **Psalm 34:1**

David and I love to read. We often find good books at thrift stores and yard sales and I am thrilled when we do. If either of us reads an especially good one, we'll compare notes as to how we felt the storyline went and what, if anything, jumped out at us.

I'd just finished reading *The Immortal*, by Angela Elwell Hunt and told David, he had to read it, too.

"The plot is different than any other book I've ever read, and there are some things we have to talk about after you've read it." Because of this, I kept asking what part he'd read and if he'd met Asher (an important character).

One morning as he read I asked, "Where are you?" He looked up from the book and said, "I'm right here!" I punched his arm.

"Where are you in the book?" He paused for a minute then answered. "This book is about other people. I'm not on any of the pages. I do know they haven't mentioned my name yet."

This time I laughed. He then said, "It's not always about me you know." and I laughed some more. Oh my, I certainly do love my husband's humour and he does love to make me laugh. It's a win-win situation, don't you think?

Sometimes it can be the silliest thing that makes someone else laugh, but oh, it is worth it. Try to bring laughter into someone's life today.

I'm Faster Than You Are!

So we may boldly say: "The LORD is my helper; I will not fear. What can man do to me?" **Hebrews 13:6**

Each evening, David and I usually walk down our gravel road and eventually end up at the creek. Then we typically turn around and go back again (uphill both ways of course). Sometimes our family comes along, and we do enjoy these times.

I think I've always loved creeks. I enjoy standing on the shores of lakes and even oceans, but there is something magical about a wooded creek. It was especially delightful for me when we purchased a small 33-acre farm with a creek meandering through the centre of the property. We often wandered down to just admire the serenity of it all.

David, Tanya, Nathan, and I love watching the creek flow and see the changes almost every time we trek down there. In the winter, the white snow clinging to the trees and the little trickle of water that forces its way through the ice is a thing of beauty. In the spring, after the winter thaw, the little creek turns into a raging torrent and we are always amazed at the damage it does to the creekbanks. Sometimes it uproots trees that have been there for decades. It is sad to see the havoc it creates.

I digress ...

On our return to the house, we saw four brown animals dart across the road at the top of the hill. I asked David what he thought they were.

"I do believe they are groundhogs and full-grown ones at that!"

David asked to stop while he leaned on my shoulder to remove a shoe.

"You have a stone in your shoe?" I asked.

"Yea, and I want to take it out in case the groundhogs attack and I have to run!"

I didn't respond, so David continued.

"Did you get what I just said? In case I have to run!"

I laughed, then, because I finally got it. "Oh my, I guess I'm a little slow."

"That's what I'm counting on dear." To his delight, I roared!

If you can't figure it out, let me know and I'll slowly explain it to you.

It does take away from the joke if the deliverer of such has to explain it, but sometimes it makes it even funnier. It feels so good to be able to laugh over something as silly as this and it does keep life interesting.

*David loves to make me laugh.
We're a good team because I laugh at his jokes.*

Beautiful Dream of my Mama

"And it shall come to pass afterward That I will pour out My Spirit on all flesh; Your sons and your daughters shall prophesy, Your old men shall dream dreams, Your young men shall see visions.
Joel 2:28

Ever since my mama died, I had been asking God for a dream or a vision of her in Heaven. It had only been two months since my precious mother's graduation there, but in many ways, it felt like two years. It's like there had been a time warp of sorts that made the traumatic events of her death seem far, far away.

One night, I had my first dream about Mom since her passing. In my dream, Janet and I were at a concert of some kind with Mom and she looked beautiful. The fact that she had on a new dress made it even more interesting because it was like no garment I had ever seen before. Of course, I made a huge fuss over it but mom, like always, just took it in stride.

Our mother always looked nice. She had a certain graceful style and took good care of her wardrobe. During the last couple of years, Janet and I had to shop for her, so it made this new outfit even more exceptional in my eyes.

In my dream, as we were listening to the entertainers, Mom shivered, so I found a shawl for her and put it around her shoulders. Although I did not remember in my dream that she had died, I do recall the feeling of utter joy to be with her. This dream puzzled me.

For a while I'd been looking forward to meeting with some fellow writers for a road trip that my publisher, Glynis Belec, had organized for us. It just so happened we were going the day after my dream. At one point I mentioned my dream to a writer friend and shared about Mom's stunning clothes. She listened to my description and said, "Perhaps you were seeing your mom in her heavenly garment." This filled me with utter joy and peace, and I exclaimed, "Yes, that is exactly it!" Although I can't recall much detail, I do remember being in awe of how Mom had looked and couldn't take my eyes off her. I don't know why she shivered, but perhaps it happened so I could do something nice for her once again by finding a shawl to lovingly place around her shoulders.

I am filled with thanksgiving that God did indeed give me a glimpse of my precious mother. It may not have been in a heavenly setting, but He allowed me to see her in a garment not of this earth.

Thank You, Father, for this glimpse of my mama in her Heavenly garment. I shall treasure it in my heart for a long, long time.

How do you feel about dreams? Do you often remember them? Some dreams are silly nonsense, but others have us pondering for a long time. Take note. Perhaps your subconscious is trying to share something with you.

Niagara Falls, Canada. August 7, 2007.
Fond memories with our Mama. Left to Right: Janet, Nancy, Jane, Mom.

Emotional Decisions

> *"Do not lay up for yourselves treasures on earth, where moth and rust destroy and where thieves break in and steal; but lay up for yourselves treasures in heaven, where neither moth nor rust destroys and where thieves do not break in and steal. For where your treasure is, there your heart will be also.* **Matthew 6:19-21**

Whenever a loved one dies, there are many details that must be addressed. Each one comes at a different time, and eventually they cannot be put off any longer and we're usually better off to get them over and done with.

One of the last things on our list was to go through Mom's clothes and personal effects. I wasn't sure how I'd feel to see all her things again, but I knew there may be tears. Surprisingly, I got through it with just a few catches in my throat. Janet assured me that it is because I have never stopped the tears when they came (and will come I'm sure) but I allowed my emotions to play themselves out until the next episode. Each time has been cleansing and I can carry on with a lighter heart.

Of course, the knowledge that Mom is with her Savior whom she loved and served all her life, has taken the sting out of my loss. Because of the difficult circumstances and her struggles with dementia at the end, we willingly released her to fly into the arms of Jesus. I knew that the angels were waiting in her room to take her Home and what a genuine relief to know her pain had ended.

Many of Mom's things were taken to the Mennonite Central Committee Thrift store for others to enjoy and we knew that the money the thrift shop made would benefit many who were in great need around the world. Mom would have approved.

Although it went very smoothly as Janet and I worked side by side making many decisions about Mom's earthly goods, it was a relief to get it done. God had a perfect time for us to dig in and do what had to be done.

After that, Hank, Janet, David, and I drove to the little town of Millbank to eat at a popular local restaurant there. They served Mennonite-style cooking and there was always a long lineup at the door. How wonderful to visit and eat delicious food with family who understood how I felt. Life was good.

There is a saying that everything that we own in life will either be given away, used up, or sold. We came into this world with nothing, and we leave it all behind. However, when we do things God's way with His direction, we are sending up treasures to heaven.

An Adorable Child

At that time the disciples came to Jesus, saying, "Who then is greatest in the kingdom of heaven?"
Then Jesus called a little child to Him, set him in the midst of them, and said, "Assuredly, I say to you, unless you are converted and become as little children, you will by no means enter the kingdom of heaven. **Matthew 18:1-3**

Kids say the cutest things!
One day I met two friends for coffee. I got there before they arrived.

While sipping my coffee I couldn't help but overhear the conversation between a little girl and her grandparents who were seated in the table behind me. I turned around to see this little one and to my delight I quickly learned quite a bit about her.

"I'm Ruby. I'm three years old." Ruby wore a cute little ladybug jacket with ears on the hood "My big sister is in school. That makes me sad 'cause I miss her." Ruby told me that she'd just eaten a smiley face cookie.

"Did that cookie make your tummy smile too?" I asked. "Yes!" she said with a giggle. She wore cute glasses, adding to her charm. Her grandparents were delightful and obviously adored their granddaughter.

After a bit, her grandpa said, "Well Pumpkin, let's go to the car, to which she replied, "I wanna drive!"

We all laughed.

"Do you know how to drive?" I asked the smiling Ruby. She answered firmly that she did! I asked her if she could see over the steering wheel or even reach the gas and the brake pedals.

"Yep!" she said with her chin up.

"Do you have a licence, Ruby?" She paused for a second. Thinking. Her face puckered up in a pout.

"Nope."

I told her that if she didn't have a licence, she could get into trouble. This set her back a bit, but she still begged her grandpa to let her drive. He said, "Well how about I drive, and you tell me the way to go." This didn't cut it. I laughed and said, "If she does drive, I'd like to see it. From a safe distance of course."

I hated to see them leave because she'd provided such good entertainment, but Ruby made sure to come to the window where I was sitting, waved a goodbye, and then walked away. A few steps later, she turned around and waved again. I think I had made a new friend that day.

My two friends came shortly after that, but, admittedly, neither Donna nor Jean were quite as cute (although they both can drive).

If you ever see this little tyke, please say hi from Nancy. Her name is Ruby, she is three, and has a ladybug coat with ears on the hood. Can't miss her!

That truly had been a magical morning for me and one that brought a smile to my face whenever I thought about it. Children have an innocence that is heart-warming, and if we take the time to listen, we can learn an awful lot. It actually brings out the child in us just to be near children and that's not a bad thing at all.

Coincidences Galore

"Ask, and it will be given to you; seek, and you will find; knock, and it will be opened to you. **Matthew 7:7**

Have you ever had a day of coincidences? Well, one day I had a ton of 'em. I woke up at 4:00 a.m. and prayed for my husband. I asked God to send us help for his sciatic-type pain that had been giving him terrible grief for over a week.

I called our doctor the following morning, but he couldn't give David an appointment right away. The next call was to our Naturopath, John Bender. Thankfully he had an opening so we could see him quickly. John sympathized greatly with David but said he needed to see a chiropractor, massage therapist, or osteopath to unlock the muscles in his back and attend to the acute pain. He went on to say that his remedies would only work after the immediate pain treatment. David sent a text to his osteopath. We were in town, so decided to stop in to visit our dear friends, Ben and Mary Jane, from church while we were waiting for the response from the osteopath. Ben just had hip surgery and Mary Jane recently lost her mother, so we wanted to visit them both, anyway.

When we arrived, another friend from church, Kate, just happened to be visiting, too, so we had a good time talking and laughing together. However, David soon had to lie on the floor to relieve the pain. Almost immediately he received a response from the osteopath. His hopeful anticipation turned to discouragement when he read the message. His osteopath texted that he was on vacation.

Kate mentioned that she worked part-time for a chiropractor. She offered to try and get David an emergency appointment. He readily agreed. With great rejoicing we were squeezed in and soon we were bidding our friends goodbye and David was under the doctor's expert care. She ordered x-rays. This doctor knew what she was doing, and soon David had relief from the agonizing pain. We stand in awe of God who arranged it all.

Our naturopath happened to have an opening that day and told David he needed a different kind of intervention than what he could offer. We happened to be visiting our friends, and Kate happened to be there, who happened to work for a chiropractor, who happened to be able to squeeze David in. That same day, there happened to be an opening for him to get x-rays right away, so we didn't need to make the trip into town again.

I had asked God for help and He sent it in many different forms, in unique ways. We stand in awe of our God who is all-knowing and who planned in advance each one of our steps. He had the answer ahead of time and made sure we were at the right places at the right times. How great our God is!

I like these anonymous quotes:

"When I stop praying, coincidences stop happening."

"Prayer is earthly license for heavenly interference."

"God does not answer every prayer the way we think He should, but there are times when He comes through in miraculous ways."

"If we don't pray, how can we expect Him to answer?"

Summer Cottage

And He said to them, "Come aside by yourselves to a deserted place and rest a while." **Mark 6:31a**

For a number of years, our daughter-in-law Sarah's brother, let our family use their cottage near Huntsville for a week. It was a beautiful spot, right on the lake with a full wall of windows overlooking a stunning view of the expansive dock. We eagerly looked forward to these times of refreshing. Nana and Bubba, as our grandchildren called us, have many cherished memories of times spent together at the cottage.

Our granddaughter, Launa, loved animals—any animals or insects (except spiders and hornets). She loved fishing too but would carefully let them go after she caught them. One day just before her eighth birthday, I asked her a question.

"Launa, do you mind letting the fish go back into the water?" I loved her reply. "I don't mind as long as I get to hold them first." I loved that she said "hold" and not just "touch." I'm sure the fish appreciated being held before they were let back into the water!

That same year, our five-year-old grandson, Trenton, found a Precious Moments® colouring book and asked me to read the captions. The one page had a picture of a sweet little old lady in a rocking chair and underneath the caption read, "God Loves Grandma." Trenton looked up me with sad eyes and said, "It doesn't say anything about Nana." His other grandma is Grandma Goetz, so I guess he figured the writers just meant her and left me out. My heart melted at his concern for Nana.

Into the third year of our cottage tradition, Matt and Sarah brought their foster daughter, Breana, along. Breana had never seen a lake before. She had also never travelled far so she was fascinated as she looked out the car window at the changing northern scenery.

When we first arrived at the cottage, we headed down to the lake. At first, Breana stayed back. She had never seen a large lake before. How huge it must have seemed to her. But it didn't take long before she waded in. Matt and Sarah gave her a life jacket and soon she was swimming and even jumping off the dock. I think she would have been totally content if we'd have thrown a sandwich to her while she floated in the lake so she wouldn't have to get out of the water to eat. We all found it interesting to see the whole cottage experience from her perspective and enjoyed ourselves even more.

We may not be a perfect family, but we do love each other, we love God, and we sure do love to laugh. Can't beat that combination.

Not everyone has access to a cottage but there are many parks, swimming pools, and forest trails to enjoy. We all need rest and relaxation, so get creative and have a day away with family and friends. You will be glad you did.

No One's Perfect

Your ears shall hear a word behind you, saying, "This is the way, walk in it," … **Isaiah 30:21a**

It is easy to put on a good front, to post happy pictures, and share flowery descriptions of a loving, well-adjusted life. But sometimes it's good to be just plain honest and tell it like it is.

David wasn't too keen when he discovered a skeleton in his closet; one of his ancestors was a bootlegger. Another ancestor had been put in prison for a serious crime. And on my side, one grandfather had an eye for the ladies, much to Grandma's chagrin. So much for perfect families.

Fact is, no one is perfect. We all have flaws and blind spots that others see but we don't. I like to give new brides the same advice I received on my wedding day: "One of the secrets of a good marriage is for both of you to be two good forgivers. After all, you both married an imperfect person."

Backgrounds are different, so it makes sense that people look at certain situations from an opposite point of view. Forgiving smooths over those differences.

I am going to be candid about a problem in our marriage in the hopes that it will encourage others to never believe that someone else has it all together.

Whenever I drive alone, I am careful to abide by the speed limit. When I'm in town, I watch ahead to see what color the light is. If it's red, I'll slow down so I won't have to actually use the brakes, but just sail through. I get a small satisfaction with my excellent timing.

David doesn't care about such things and I'm constantly saying, "The light just turned red" or "Did you see the light?" Although (to my credit), I don't always say something, I still think of the harm it's doing to the brakes and the extra expense in gas that could be avoided. David often gets upset with me, but I bravely keep on "doing my duty."

One Sunday it came to a head. I had pointed out a light change and he said, "You know Nancy, if there was one thing about our marriage that I hate and would change, it's your backseat driving."

I got quiet and contemplated David's cutting words. Oh dear. Did he actually hate my observations this much? Apparently. However, I didn't learn my lesson, but had to add my two cents worth on the drive home.

"Do you want to drive?" David's tone caught me off guard.

Oops! Well, the answer to that was a resounding "No."

David was a good driver and really didn't need my advice. I am happy to let my husband battle traffic so I can look at the scenery (and watch for red lights). His stern reprimand that day wasn't easy to ignore, though. It felt like a dose of cold water tossed in my face.

I'd like to say I am a reformed back seat driver but occasionally I digress. However, you'll be happy to know, I'm doing a whole lot better, and I am trying.

"David, did you see ..."

I like this George R.R. Martin quote from his book, *A Feast for Crows* with a slight change to the name: "Words are like arrows, [Nancy]. Once loosed, you cannot call them back."

Good advice, don't you think?

Hero!

... For everyone to whom much is given, from him much will be required; ... **Luke 12:48b**

I was hailed as a hero! Well ... maybe not a hero exactly, more like a ... well ... I'll let you decide.

There I was in the grocery store minding my own business. David was in a different part of the store and I was checking out the dairy section when all of a sudden, I saw something big and black out of the corner of my eye. When I realized what it was, my heart nearly stopped, and I yelped. I tell you—it was a HUMONGOUS black bird! Well ... perhaps I'm exaggerating just a little bit. It may not have been humongous, but it *was*, at the very least, a man-eating bird and it scared the living daylights out of me. It disappeared from my view, but when I went around the corner, the attack bird reappeared and once again I let out a yelp, except louder this time, which caused an employee to poke his head over one of the shelves. He must have been kneeling to fill the bottom shelf and when he asked what was wrong, I pointed and shakily said, "A bird!"

My knight in shining armour took two cardboard boxes and captured the monster and then called for the manager. He was laughing and said, "Wait until I tell him about this!" When the manager came, he asked how the employee captured it, and he gallantly said, "This lady screamed, and I boxed it." I then told the manager what a hero his employee was for catching it, and my "knight" said, "No, WE captured it!" (how gallant) "All I did was alert you with my screams," I said, but he insisted that I was a huge help.

Somehow, word got out that I was the one who screamed about the bird and one of the employees came and said, "Thanks so much for helping catch that bird. It must have flown in yesterday. I worked the night shift but didn't see hide nor hair of it. In fact, we called Animal Control, but now the office can cancel that call thanks to you!"

To make it even better, when we went to the checkout counter, David told the cashier (who we knew) and she laughed and called me a hero. To be fair, I've never been called a hero before, and I admit that my chest did swell a little under the praise.

Of course, all I did was scream and gain a few more gray hairs and almost had a heart attack, but hey, I saved the day at the grocery store. I can see the headline now: "Nancy Seiling Saves the Day by Taking on Humongous Black Bird in Local Grocery Store. News at 11:00."

I think I'll take my Supergirl cape off now because that was enough excitement for one day! Like David's Uncle used to say, "Why let a story get dull for lack of information?"

Do you have a funny story to tell? It may not be as "heroic" as mine but take a risk and share it. You'll be surprised at how it could brighten someone's day and cause a memory to surface in their minds. Soon you may find yourself having a good belly laugh together which is extremely healthy for many reasons.

Confession is Good for the Soul

If we confess our sins, He is faithful and just to forgive us our sins and to cleanse us from all unrighteousness. **1 John 1:9**

I have a confession to make. I often jump to conclusions. Recently I heard someone complained about me. At first, I was hurt, then filled with anger. Poor David had to listen to my ranting and raving.

"Aren't you glad I'm not mad at you?" I said in between my performance. He just smiled and said, "Well, yea!"

I was certain that I knew why someone complained about me, but I felt (no … I knew) I was in the right and how dare they complain? On and on I went until I had to cry out to the Lord to help me settle down. And He did.

Then a few days later I was reading my friend, Angelina Fast-Vlaar's book, *Bring Each Other Home*[5]. In one chapter, Angelina recalls a time when someone attacked her and she responded with these words, "No matter how others act, it is never an excuse for me to not be clothed with compassion, kindness, humility, gentleness, and patience." A good adaptation of Colossians 3:12.

That hit me like a two by four. I wrote the ugly mess down in my prayer journal and confessed my lousy attitude to God and felt His cleansing.

Then something else triggered my memory and I felt the rage trying to bubble up again. So, I bowed my head and prayed that God would help me in that struggle, too. I knew I was powerless on my own and soon His peace flooded me once again and I carried on.

A few days later I found out what really happened. Apparently, the people who I was sure complained about me, never did. It was just a request to ask for my opinion on a difficult problem because I was in charge of this department. Oh dear! Well, this put a whole new spin on things, and I hung my head.

---

[5] Fast-Vlaar, Angelina. Bring Each Other Home. Winnipeg, Manitoba, Word Alive Press, 2019.

I learned a huge lesson that day. *Nancy, do not get all hot and bothered and make poor David listen to your tirade until you have all the information.* Had I simply waited for clarification, there would have been no "storm," and it would have been an interesting conversation. But did Nancy do that? "No!" Has Nancy learned her lesson? I truly hope so.

From experience I can honestly say, wait until all the facts are in. Do not try to guess what the other person meant, for you could be looking at it through a faulty filter. If this helps even one person, then it is worth putting this whole sorry mess down for everyone to see.

My long-suffering hubby

Backpack vs. Boulders

Bear one another's burdens, and so fulfill the law of Christ. For each one shall bear his own load. **Galatians 6:2,5**

When I was ill with Chronic Fatigue Syndrome, I read verses two and five of Galatians, Chapter 6 and was deeply troubled. Here I was, barely able to get out of bed yet God expected me to carry my own load and everyone else's burdens? This almost pushed me into despair.

Then I read this explanation: In life, figuratively speaking, we are all given a backpack. In this backpack are stones of troubles. As we get older, the backpack gets heavier if we don't deal with the problems head-on. Our backpacks are ours and ours alone to deal with.

Occasionally, a boulder comes along; a boulder far too heavy for us to carry alone. We must have help or we will crumble beneath the load.

Trouble comes when some refuse to carry their own backpack. They expect others to not only carry their own personal backpack but add theirs as well to the pile. They somehow feel that they are the only one with a backpack, so therefore, someone else should carry it for them. They do not care that they are burdening the other person greatly. They feel entitled and then relieved to get rid of their problems.

Then there are the ones who are too proud or too stubborn to even ask for help with their boulder. It could be they do not feel they should burden others with their problems. Perhaps they can't even admit there is a boulder. They struggle unnecessarily through life and become crippled from trying.

Both scenarios are wrong and unhealthy and will damage us in many ways. This is where we need God to help us decide which is which. Am I unwilling to carry my own load? Am I too stubborn to accept help with something that is beyond my capacity to carry? Sometimes by thinking I am helping someone, I may, in fact, be hindering their growth. This may circumvent God's plan.

Which camp would say you were in? Do you ask for help for even the smallest problem or do you refuse any help at all? Neither scenario is healthy. Ask God to help you make good decisions in your life to neither smother (don't enable) nor shun (don't totally ignore) those in your life who may truly need your help.

Fear not, for I am with you; Be not dismayed, for I am your God. I will strengthen you, Yes, I will help you, I will uphold you with my righteous right hand.
Isaiah 41:10

During my dark, lonely years, I would gaze at pictures like these. It gave me hope that the future would some day be brighter. And it was.

Chance Meeting

Your word is a lamp to my feet And a light to my path.
Psalm 119:105

I have to smile when I see how God uses ordinary things to make sure we are at the right place at the right time for a special encounter.

One day I decided to visit my friend Lovada while David played hockey at a local park. I dropped David off and drove to Lovada's home.

My plan had been to get back to the park before David got off the ice, walk a few rounds on the inside track, and then join him so we could enjoy lunch together. My stomach growled when I arrived back at the park and pulled out our lunch. *Just eat a quarter of your sandwich and get walking Nancy.* So, I did. A quarter turned into a half, then three quarters. Before I knew it, I had gulped the entire sandwich down along with a whole pear. David would soon come out, so I didn't get to walk, either. I felt rather disgusted with myself because I chose to eat rather than walk.

David ate his lunch while I told him about my morning and my appetite that kept me from walking. He suggested we walk a few rounds together. On our journey we saw an older woman sitting on a bench and we sort of locked eyes and we smiled at each other.

"My husband and I used to walk here," she said. We stopped to talk because I recognized her from somewhere. We told her our names, but she didn't change expression. Even saying we were ventriloquists didn't work (it usually does).

She told us her name was Martha. "Mel and I organized bus tours for years."

"That's it!" I said. I knew I recognized her from somewhere. "I went on an overnight tour with you for part of my training with the tour company."

She didn't remember me, but I would never forget that tour. Working as a bus tour guide was my favourite job. How could I forget?

Then two other women walked toward us. Martha introduced them as her daughters. They recognized us right away remembering our involvement in our musical groups, The Dubrick Sisters and The Joyful Sound from way back.

Suddenly I thought about my latest book (*When is Tomorrow? A Devotional for Caregivers*) and ran to get it from the car. I've learned to always carry copies with me just in case someone is interested, and it certainly worked out this time. The two girls were thrilled because they were caregivers for their mom and bought the book on the spot. We continued walking, and each time we passed Martha we couldn't help but notice her flipping through the pages of my book.

"I'm going to enjoy this for sure!" she'd say.

So, there you have it. God used my appetite to make sure I didn't walk alone so David and I could walk past Martha later and then meet her daughters who bought my book for their mom and themselves. The timing was perfect.

God did it again!

Sometimes God has us change direction because He knows where we are to be at the right time. That means, even though we might feel it is a mistake, He knows best. Do you have a story of where you thought things weren't turning out only to have it revealed that God had a much better plan? If so, tell someone. It will increase their faith and yours too.

Civic Duty

Honor all people. Love the brotherhood. Fear God. Honor the king. **1 Peter 2:17**

David had an unusual 70th birthday. In fact, neither David nor I have ever heard of someone spending their 70th birthday this way.

Our country was headed for a federal election. Some of our friends who attended the same church as us, were heavily involved in the process. They asked a few of us if we'd be willing to help on election day. Once we found out that David and I could work at the same station, we agreed, even though it was his birthday. It also helped that many of our friends were at the same polling booth, so in the lulls we could visit back and forth.

Years before I had helped on election day, but it had not been a good experience. My partner seemed to have had a chip on her shoulder right from the beginning so when one small mistake happened it set off a barrage of problems.

Instead of working together on the problem, she went home after the polls closed and left me alone to sort it out. I had to call David to drive me to the main polling station to do so. I decided right then and there I would never help at a polling station again.

However, this time we were committed and since David and I could be together at our polling station, it made the decision to say yes, a whole lot easier. We had to attend an intensive training session, stand in long lines to pick up our huge packets with all the paraphernalia we needed, and spend the next 15 hours doing our duty on election day.

I would have baked a birthday cake for David but that seemed awkward, so I made a huge batch of my chocolate popcorn instead. The "Birthday Popcorn" became an instant hit. I made sure to tell all the other workers we were celebrating David's birthday. Most of them loved it and came back for more.

All went well until the polls closed. Our ballots and numbers balanced, but when it came time to put everything in the proper bags, something was amiss. The numbers were so much the same:

3782265-3 and, 3782265-4 and on and on. We were exhausted from the long day and our brains were fried. Finally, we asked for help and were the last ones out. When we fell into the car, we looked at each other and said, "Never again." And this time we meant it!

However, David does have bragging rights on where he spent his 70th birthday, and for our family, that's all that counts!

Do you celebrate birthdays? Can you remember one that is most memorable, even if it wasn't pleasant? Sometimes it's O.K. to talk about it and perhaps it won't look so bad in retrospect. You may even give someone a chuckle or two.

Twenty years earlier on David's 50th birthday.

Being Honest

Sanctify them by Your truth. Your word is truth. **John 17:17**

"Other than that, I'm fine John." These are the words I uttered to my Naturopath in his office one day when I went in for a treatment for some pain I'd been having in my jaw. Fortunately, David came with me and it shocked him when I uttered those six words to John. He frowned.

"Nancy, how can you say that you are fine? Now tell John what is really going on."

This piqued John's interest and he sat back in his chair. "Okay, Nancy, tell me everything."

The tears were close to the surface as I recounted all the different stresses in my life and how I felt as if I was slipping back into Chronic Fatigue Syndrome. That horrified me.

I couldn't believe that I would glibly tell John I was fine when I wasn't. Truth is, I am so used to putting on a happy, smiley, "everything is perfectly fine" face, that at that moment I truly felt everything else was fine. Had David not been there, John would never have known the truth.

"Anything else you need to tell me, Nancy?" he asked.

"Well, I do have nightmares."

"Tell me about them," he urged.

"My nightmares, lately, usually have something to do with Elections Canada. I sense there is still something left undone and I feel frantic trying to figure out what it is."

John nodded. He urged me to go on.

"Then I wake up with a pounding heart." I told John how I talked myself down, reminding myself that the job was over.

David remained quiet. I continued to share how I used my journal to help me work through some things. I told John that writing helped me deal with problems and I usually felt better after pouring my fears and concerns onto the page. God knows more about me than I know about myself but writing it in long-hand helped me sort things out.

So, I was a very thankful gal. Thankful that my husband just happened to go with me to my appointment. And to John, always a good listener, who gave me remedies to help me carry on.

"Do you feel better after talking with John?" David asked on the drive home after the appointment.

"Yes, I do, and I thank you for jumping in when you did."

Great day all around and, even though it was wet and dreary outside, I do believe a little sunshine glimmered within that day.

Do you have someone you can honestly confide in? Perhaps it's a family member, a friend, a minister, or a priest. The important thing is to be honest and get your concerns out into the open. When we hold things in, they grow in intensity and often become distorted. If you don't feel as if you can talk about it, tell God all about it, or write it down and be totally honest. The important thing is not to bury it. We can try to bury emotions, but they never really die until we deal with them. And usually, they will pop up at the most inopportune time.

How Did Tomorrow Become Yesterday?

But now, O LORD, You are our Father; We are the clay, and You our potter; And all we are the work of Your hand. **Isaiah 64:8**

I have a tendency to be emotional. Tears spring without too much provocation sometimes. They usually aren't sad tears, mind you, but more often, tears of wonderment and thankfulness to God for all He has done for me. A song, a poem, or even a word can cause me to suddenly well up.

This happened to me recently when I found a box of old photographs. A sweet walk down memory lane. There were images of my grandparents and parents in their younger years; the smiling faces of my sisters and me when we were kids; pictures of when our boys were young. David had thick black hair, and I used to be thin. My how things have changed.

One photograph of Grandma, my Mom, Janet, Jane, and me in the long-term care home where Grandma lived, really jumped out at me. Sometimes we'd visit as The Dubrick Sisters and put on a program for the residents. In the picture, we were crowded around Grandma with her walker and we all wore huge smiles. The thought came to me that years later, Janet and I would be with Mom and her walker, and it made me cry. Our sister Jane had gone to Heaven a couple of years earlier, so Janet and I took turns visiting Mom daily, just like she visited her mother in long-term care.

Mom always looked and acted youthful. She was active and energetic, hosting countless dinners where she'd serve her famous succulent roast beef. Anyone who tasted her meals in the past would have fond memories of them. She rode her bicycle until she turned 80 years old and only gave it up because she had a nasty fall and it frightened her.

To witness Mom's rapid decline in her mid and late 80s was painful, and to stand helplessly by while her mind also declined into dementia broke our hearts.

When Mom's legs gave out and she had to be in a wheelchair, it disturbed Janet and me. We would never have dreamed that Mom's last years would be so challenging for her.

This made me wonder what I will be like in 20 or more years. Will my children surround me and my walker in long-term care? Watching Mom's decline makes me pray that God will take me home before that happens, but some things are beyond our control.

God is sovereign and knows the date of our birth and the date of our death. Until then, I want my life to count for Him. I want to live each day to the fullest and be thankful for the many blessings God has given us.

There is a song I truly love, "I Know Who Holds Tomorrow."[6]

We may not be able to peer into the future, but we can have peace knowing God knows what is ahead and is preparing us for it.

Our favourite photo of us performing at a wedding reception.

---

[6] "I Know Who Holds Tomorrow; Ira F. Stanphill; Lyrics © Warner Chappell Music, Inc.

Covid-19

The LORD is my light and my salvation; Whom shall I fear? The LORD is the strength of my life; Of whom shall I be afraid?
Psalm 27:1

I'm sure that I am not alone saying that the restrictions of COVID-19 came upon us quickly. One Sunday we were meeting at church and the next Sunday we couldn't. Stores, restaurants, and businesses were shut down and we were all warned to stay home. Suddenly life as we knew it was taken from us and we could do nothing about it.

Gas prices were the lowest they had been in years, but, like most people, our car sat in the driveway day after day. Grocery shopping once a week seemed to be the only outing we made. However, we were thankful that stores kept up with the demand most of the time, but it was sobering to sometimes see empty shelves. Our society had been used to having everything at our fingertips and now shortages were appearing.

We heard of many who were filled with anxiety, but I could honestly say that we never were. It had nothing to do with us of course, but over the years we learned that God is our Father, and He will take care of us. He has proven His faithfulness over the years and we simply trusted that He had the pandemic situation under control, and still does. What peace we have in the midst of this storm and our hearts are full of thanksgiving.

David and I fared well because we had each other and we both enjoyed reading. I loved finding good Christian books at thrift stores and yard sales, so we had a full personal library. Soon we had a large pile of books we'd finished reading and decided to donate them to a church that offered drive-in-services once the weather warmed up. At first, we couldn't get out of our cars after the service, but eventually we were allowed to visit with others at a distance, and it felt wonderful.

Gradually, the rules have relaxed a little, and life has returned to somewhat normal once again. As of this writing, we still are required to wear masks and I must say we both find masks most difficult, so we stay away from as many public places as possible.

Through it all, the pandemic has brought us closer and more thankful than ever for all the blessings God has given us. We have lots of food in our cupboards and plenty of fresh air outside to go for walks whenever we wish.

We may not know what the future holds, but we sure do know Who holds the future.

Long ago family gathering. Good times.

Win a prize!
Simply name each member of the Dubrick Sisters' families in order of birth, their age, and their weight at the time this picture was taken. The grand prize will be an all-expense paid trip to lovely downtown Elora. Operators are standing by.

What is Ahead?

... being confident of this very thing, that He who has begun a good work in you will complete it until the day of Jesus Christ;
Philippians 1:6

Although David and I are now in our early 70s we certainly do not feel it. I've heard that inside every old person is a young person who is shocked at the face that stares back at them in the mirror. It's true!

Neither of us is ready to just sit back and retire completely. We have no idea if God still has something big for us to do. Or perhaps our call is just to be good parents, grandparents, siblings, and friends to those in our circle.

We know we'd be welcomed back to Hong Kong anytime and would be delighted to go. However, we would have to be sure that God indeed is opening that door, for it is not for the faint of heart.

Truth is, we don't have to do huge things for God. He has given each of us talents and gifts and is only asking that we simply listen to His voice and obey whatever He asks. When we are living God's way and with His direction, wonderful things happen. Tasks won't be a burden but a joy. Even the little acts of obedience will bear much fruit and we will feel contentment and fulfillment.

So, no matter what your talents are, use them to the fullest. Be thankful for each day and be open to God's leading. Rejoice that God has you in the palm of His hand and delights in YOU!

I love the chorus, "Little is much when God is in it." It just may surprise us in Heaven someday when many obscure but faithful saints will receive the greatest accolades. God looks at our hearts and will reward us accordingly.

I leave you with this anonymous, inspirational quote: "Don't feel like you gotta do it all. Just let Jesus use you where you are."

2021. Front row: Nathan, Tyson (the dog), Trenton, Breana.
Back row: Samara, Taylor, Tanya, David, Nancy, Matt, Sarah, Launa.

About the Author

Nancy Seiling's first book, *When Is Tomorrow?* centres around her mother's struggle with dementia. She thought it would be her one and only book, but little did she know at the time, God thought differently. He laid it on Nancy's heart that she had a second book brewing. As Nancy is typically wont to do, she listened and obeyed, and this book is the result of her obedience.

Nancy, and her husband David, live in a lovely country home located in the heart of a farming community in Southwestern Ontario, although she doesn't profess to be a farmer. Don't ask her to drive a tractor, either, because you might not see her for weeks (unless it has a GPS). And shovelling out stalls? Well let's just say she cooks a mean roast beef.

Both Nancy and David are not only head over heels in love with each other, they are head over heels happy about what God has done in their lives over the years. To say the least, their adventures have been interesting. They have travelled extensively in ministry using ventriloquism, music, drama, and stories, and they both love to share their adventures and the faithfulness of their Lord.

They are proud parents of two grown sons, they are thankful for their two beautiful daughters-in-law, and are devoted to their five grandchildren. None of them mind tractors or shovelling. For that, Nancy is grateful.

You can find Nancy on Facebook or you can contact her at nancy@povertysim.com.

Another Publication by Nancy Seiling:

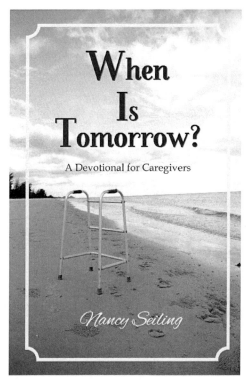

ISBN: 978-1-988155-22-7
$20

Signed copies available by contacting the author at
nancy@povertysim.com

Look Nancy up on Facebook
https://www.facebook.com/nancy.seiling.3

Also available on www.amazon.ca